Crystal Meadows

COLORING BOOK

A Relaxing Return to Nature

Sigita Alekne

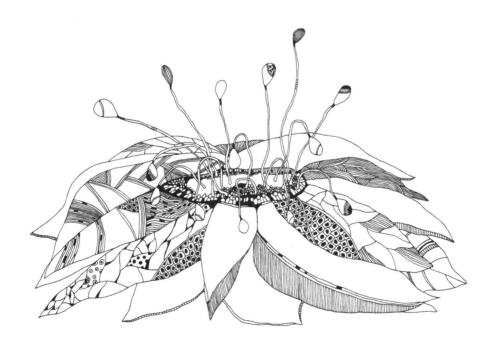

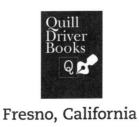
Quill Driver Books

Fresno, California

Crystal Meadows Coloring Book
Copyright ©2016 by Sigita Alekne. All rights reserved.

Published by Quill Driver Books,
an imprint of Linden Publishing

2006 South Mary, Fresno, California 93721
559-233-6633 / 800-345-4447
QuillDriverBooks.com

Quill Driver Books and Colophon
are trademarks of Linden Publishing, Inc.

ISBN 978-1-61035-285-7

Printed in the United States
First Printing
Library of Congress Cataloging-in-Publication Data on file

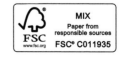

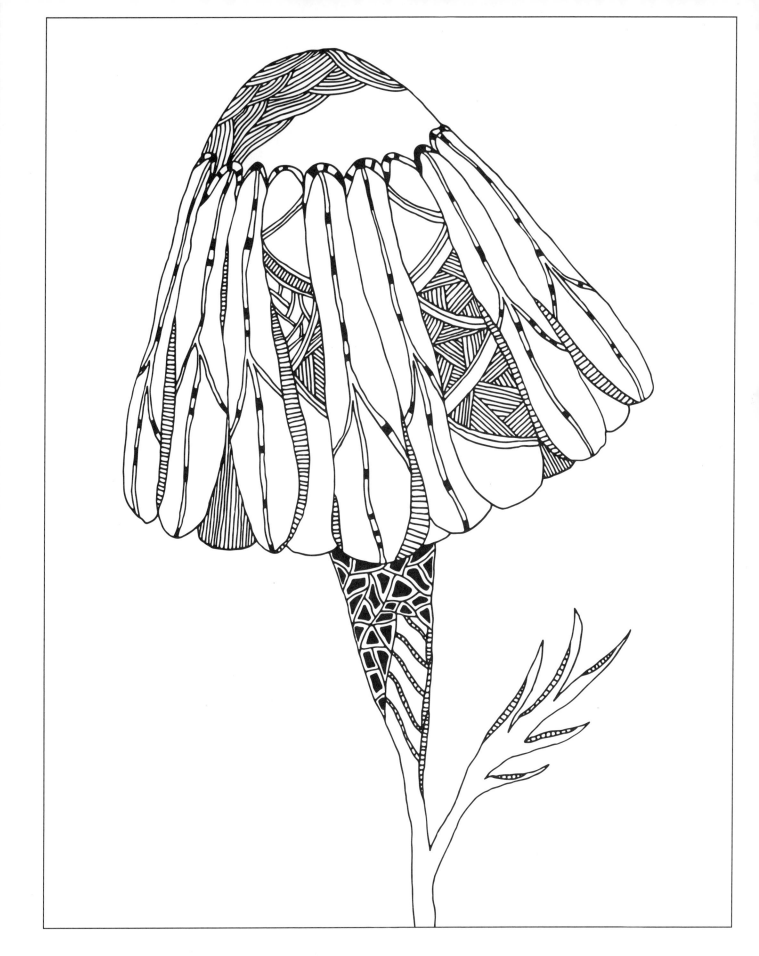

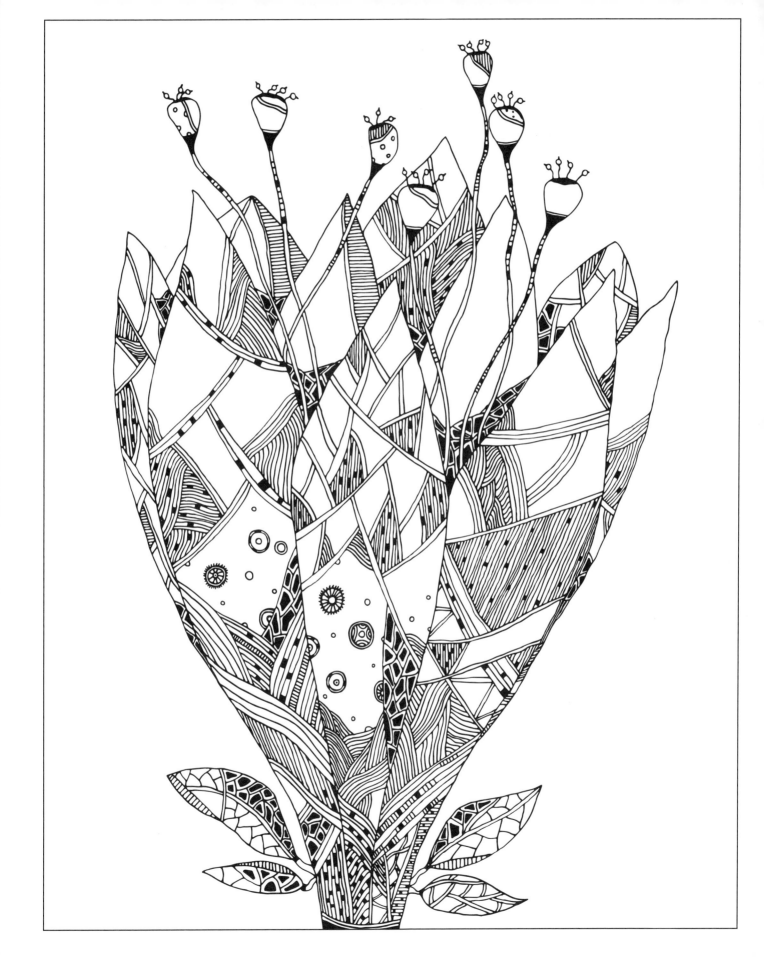

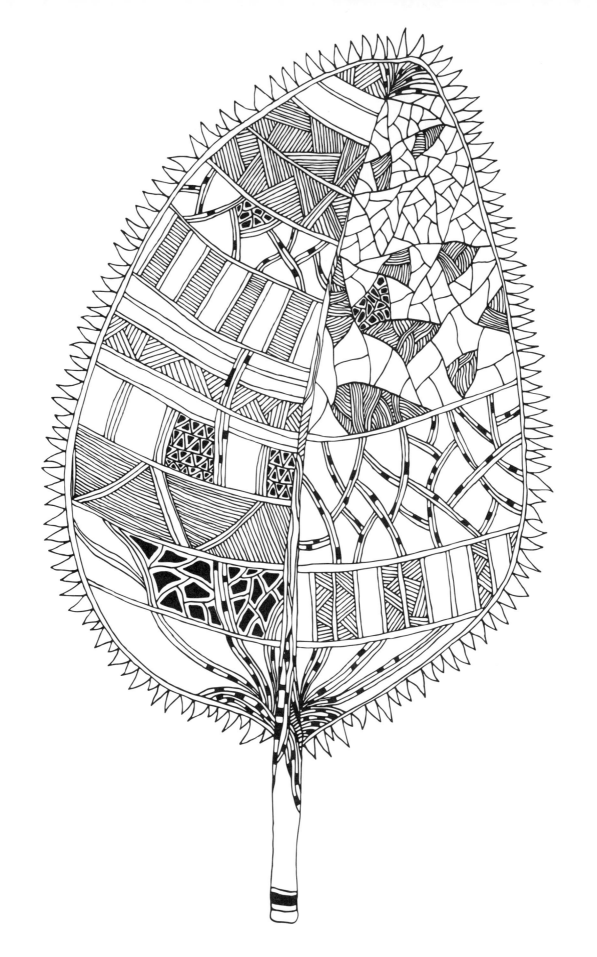

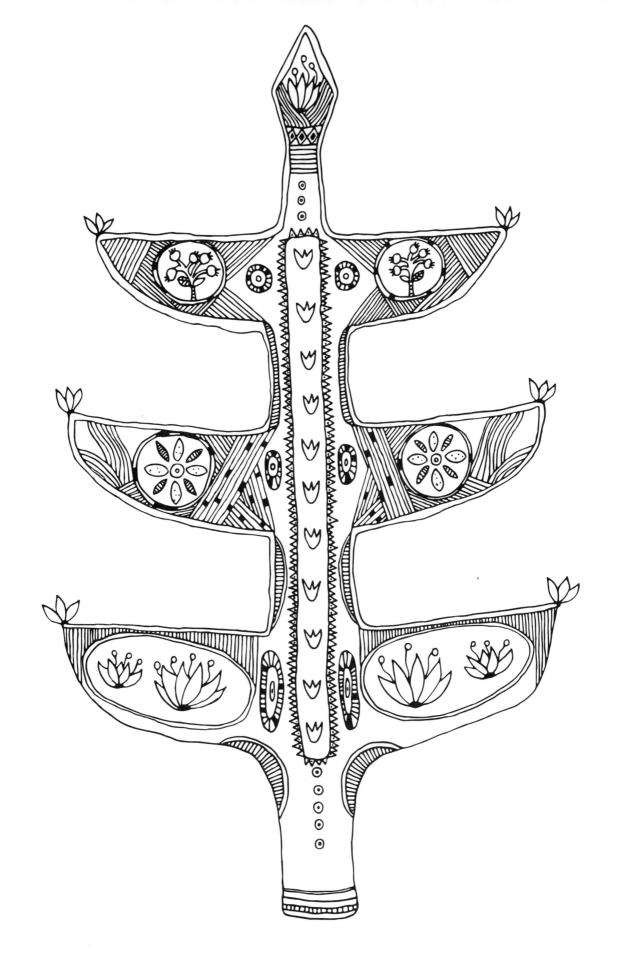

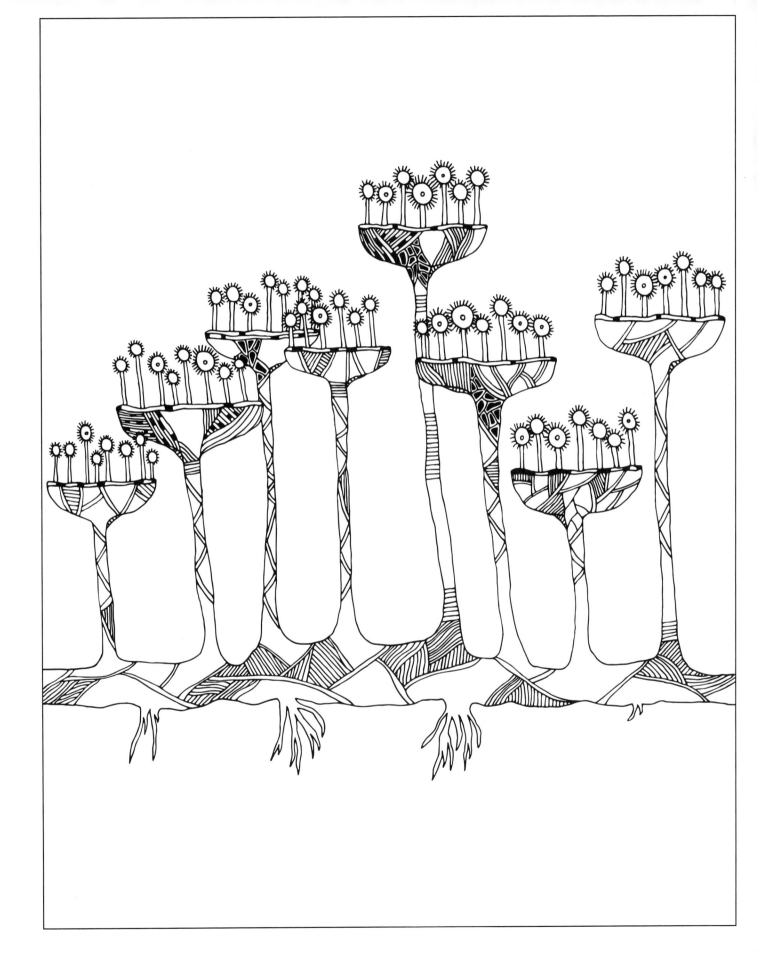

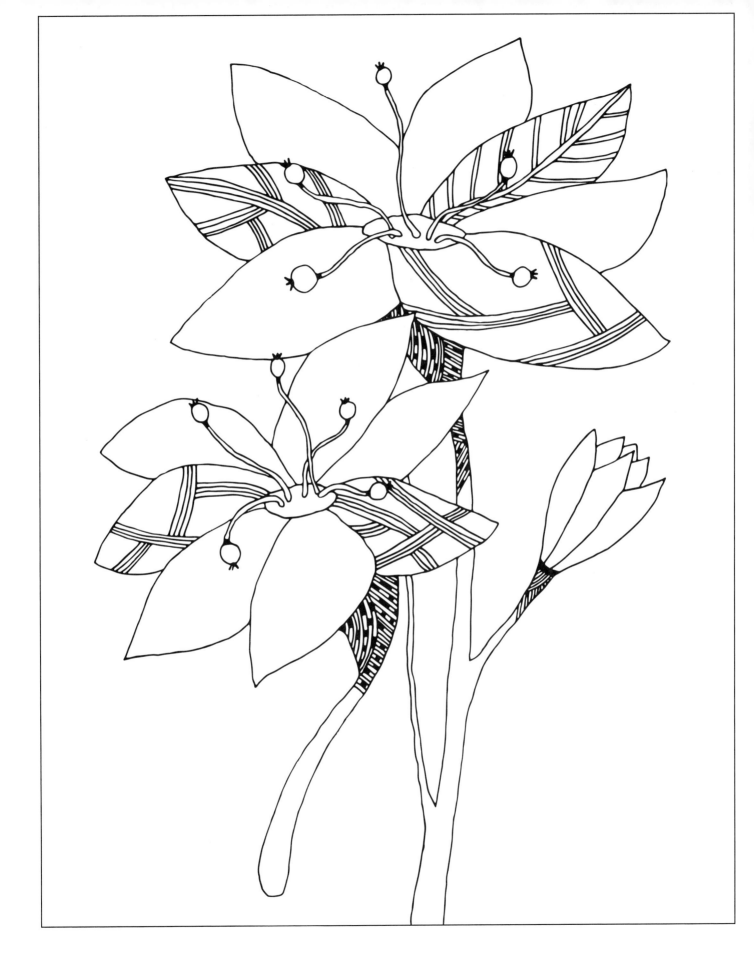

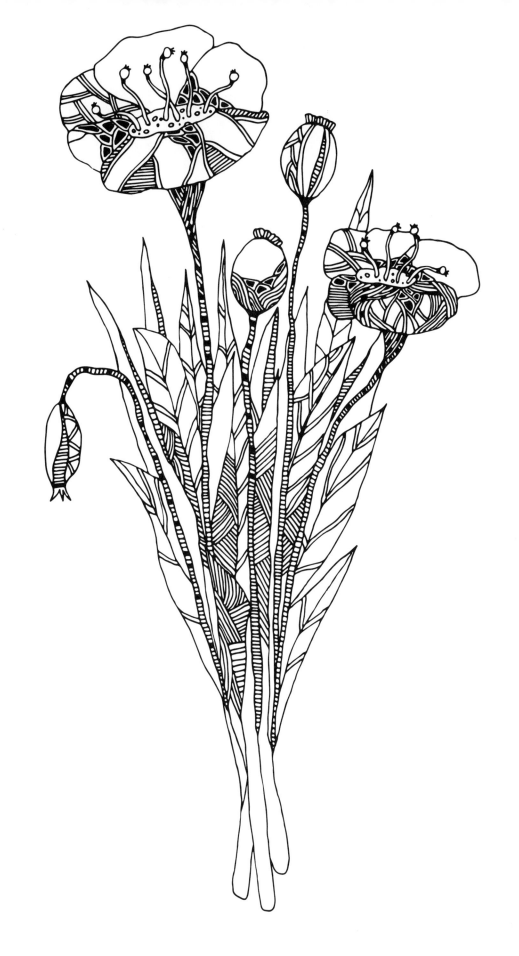

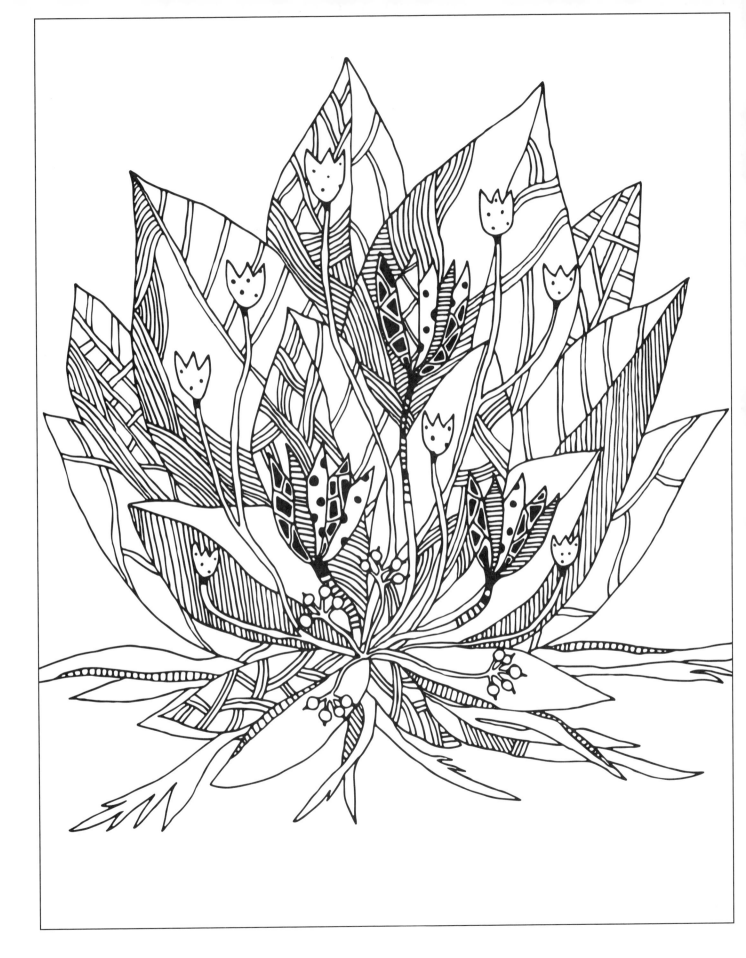

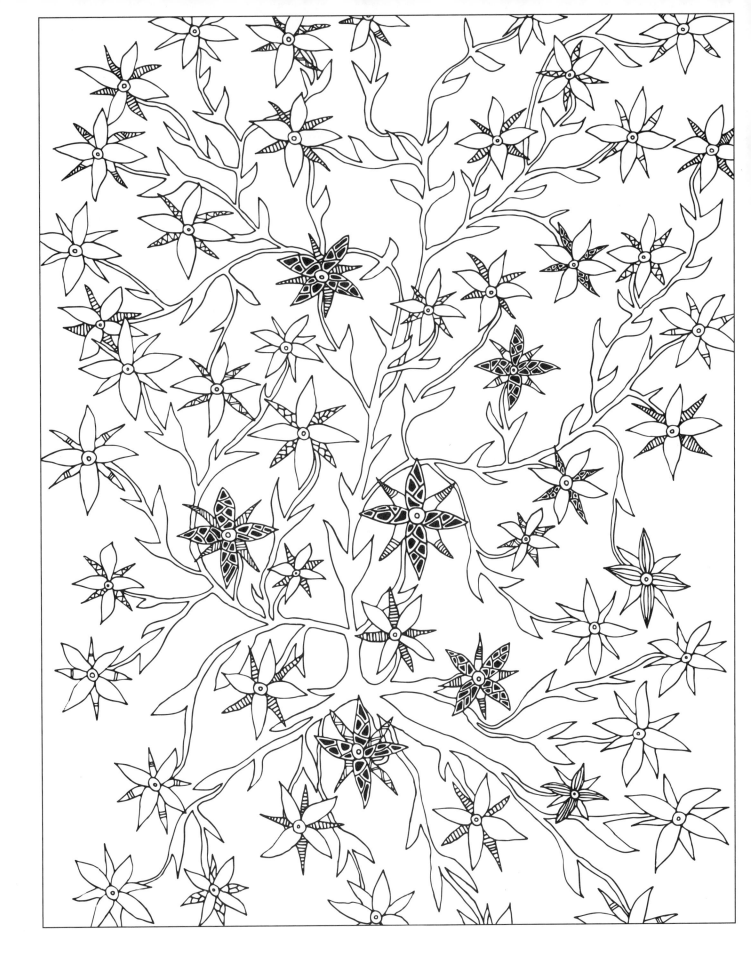

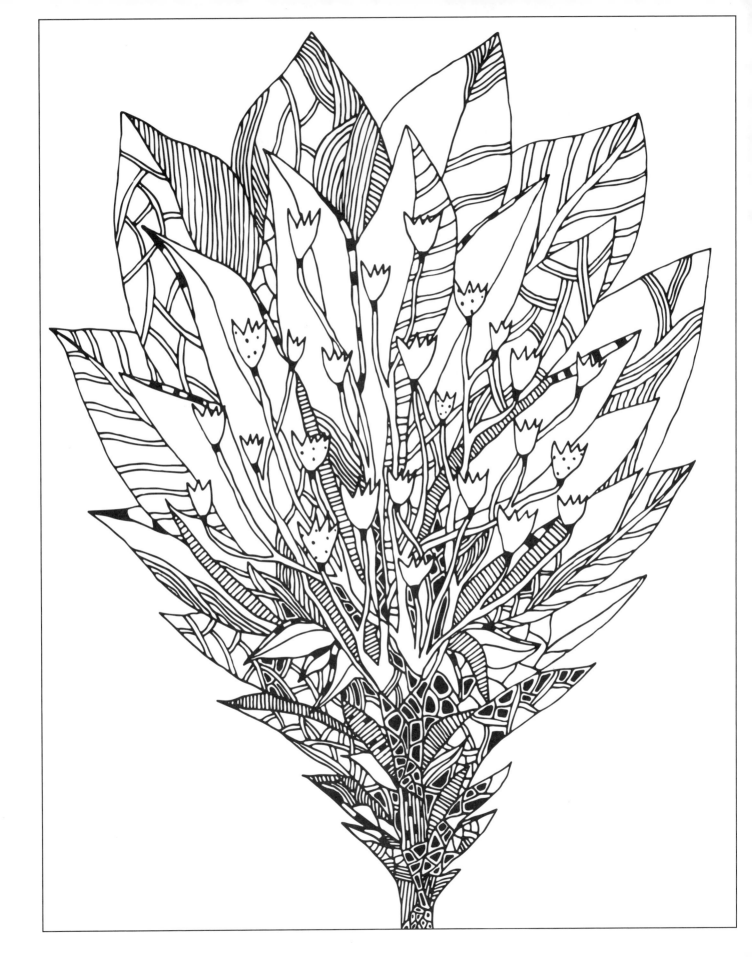

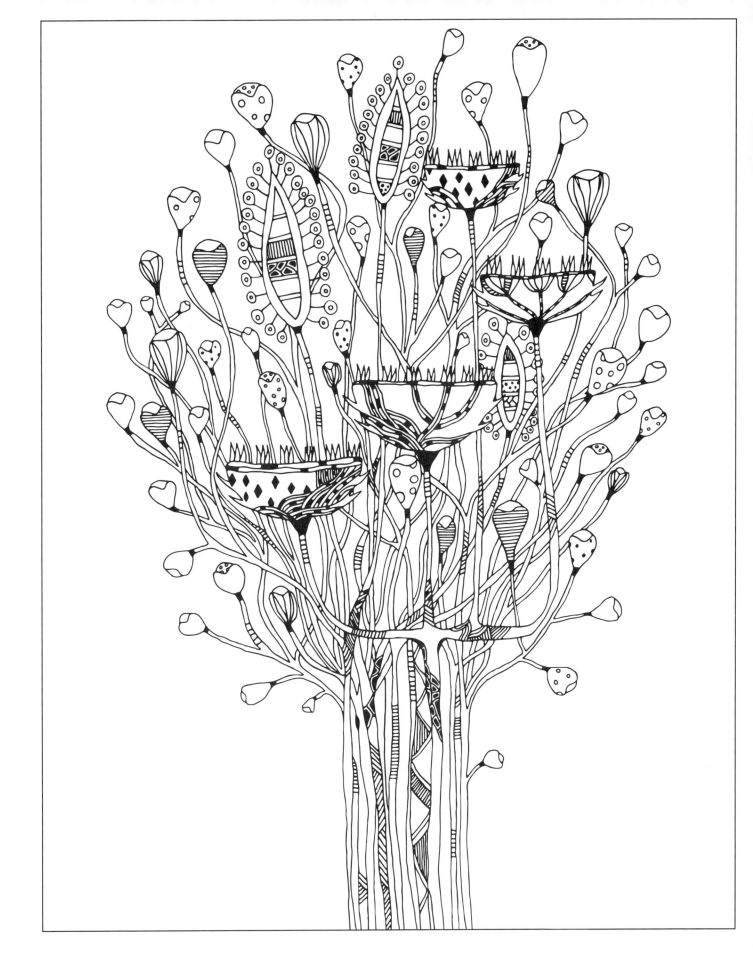

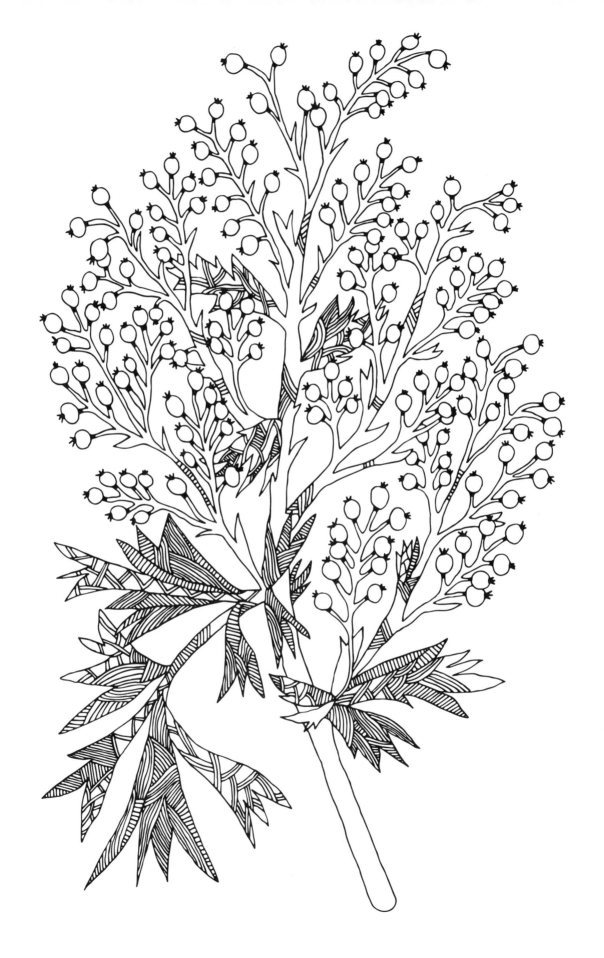

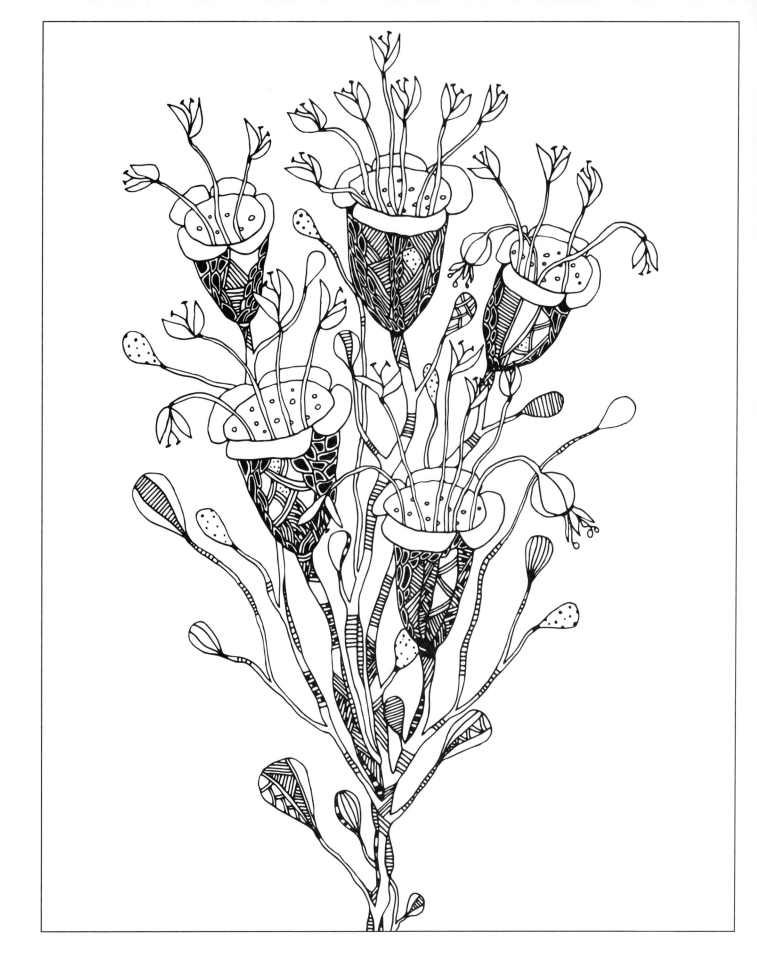

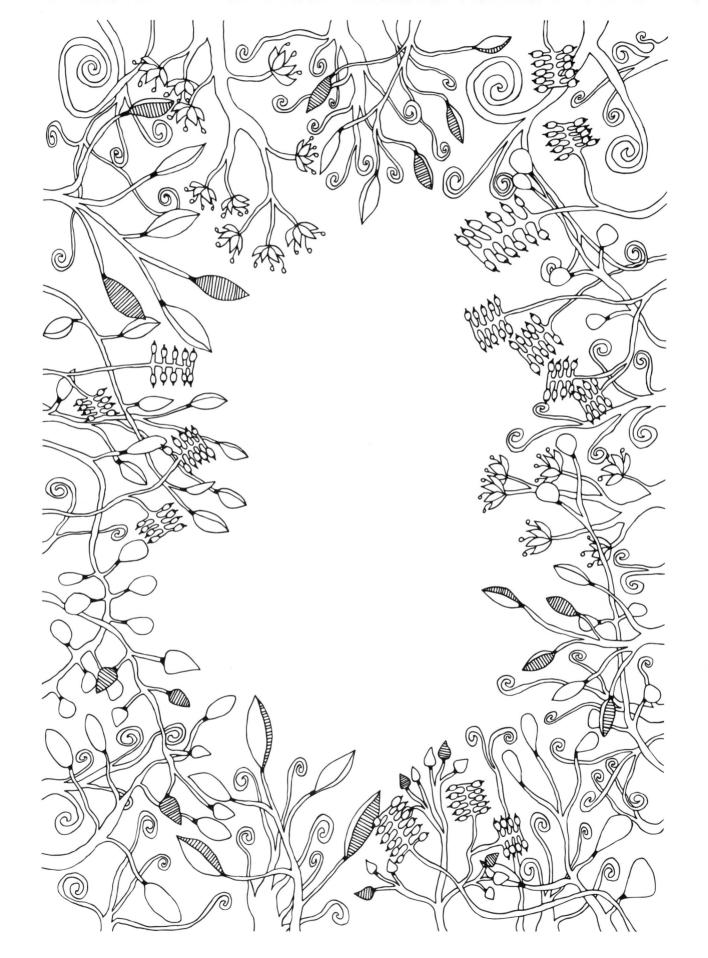

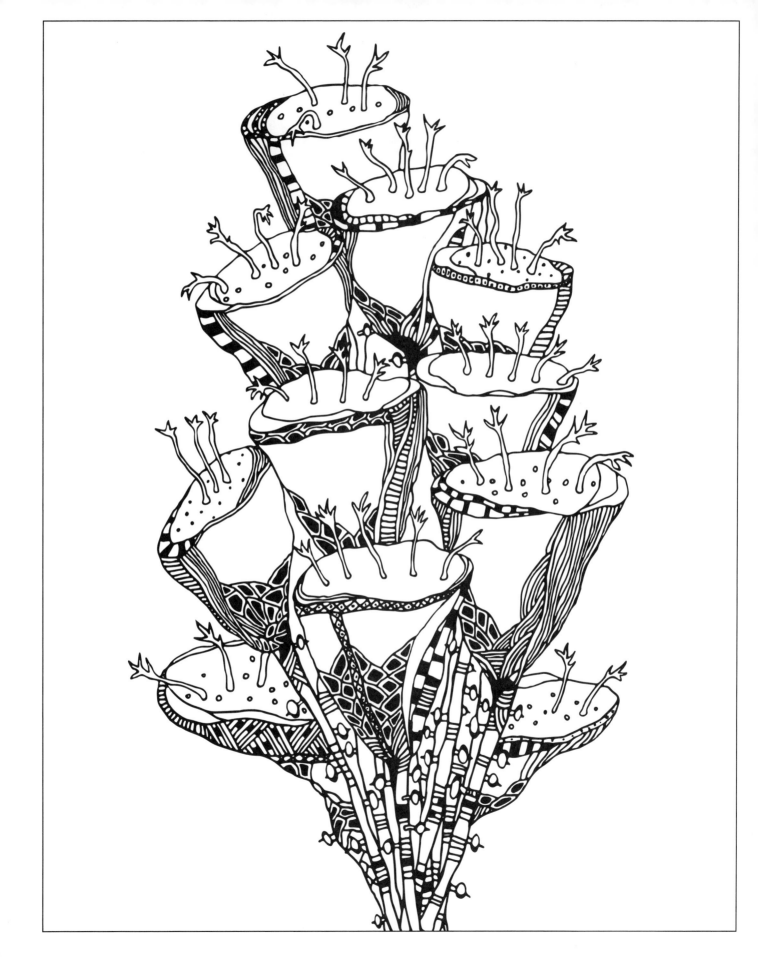

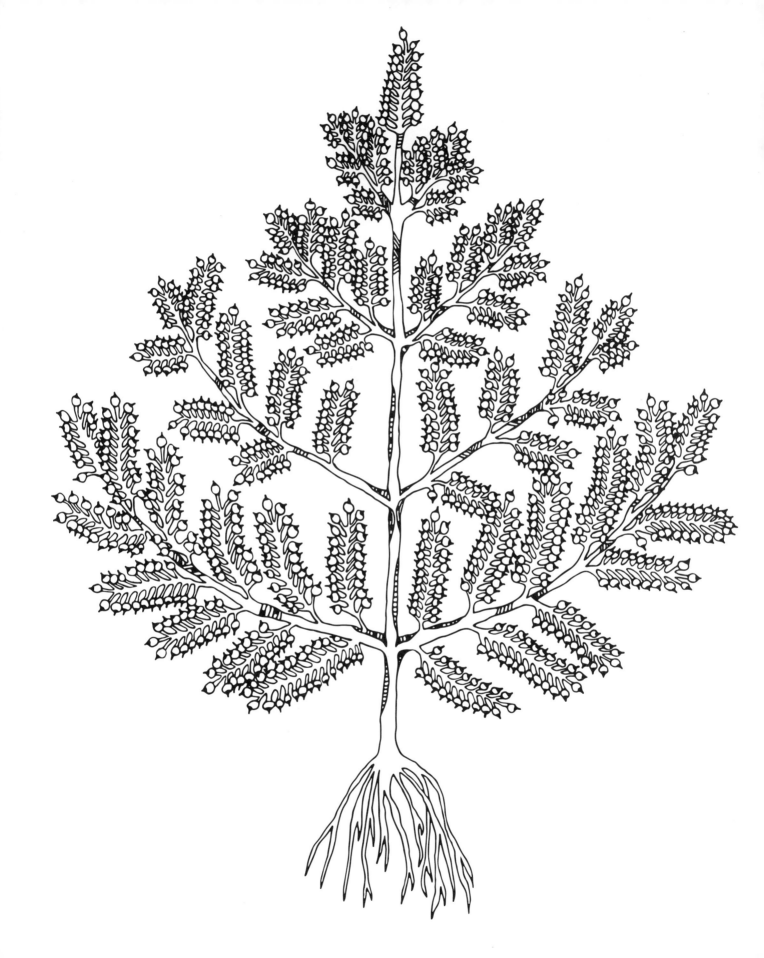

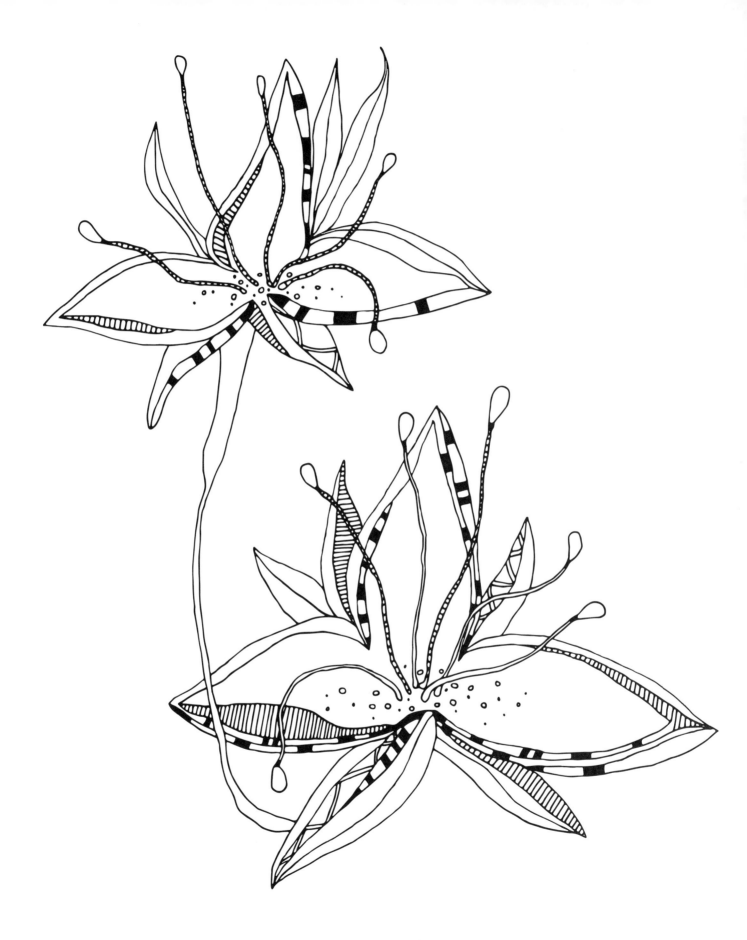

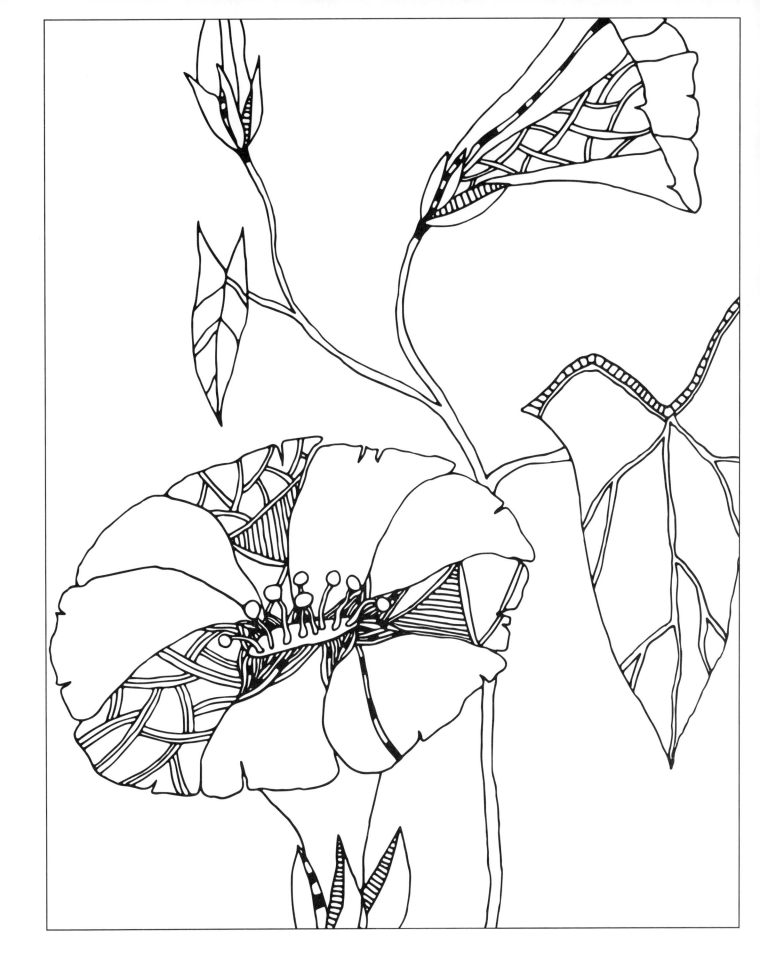

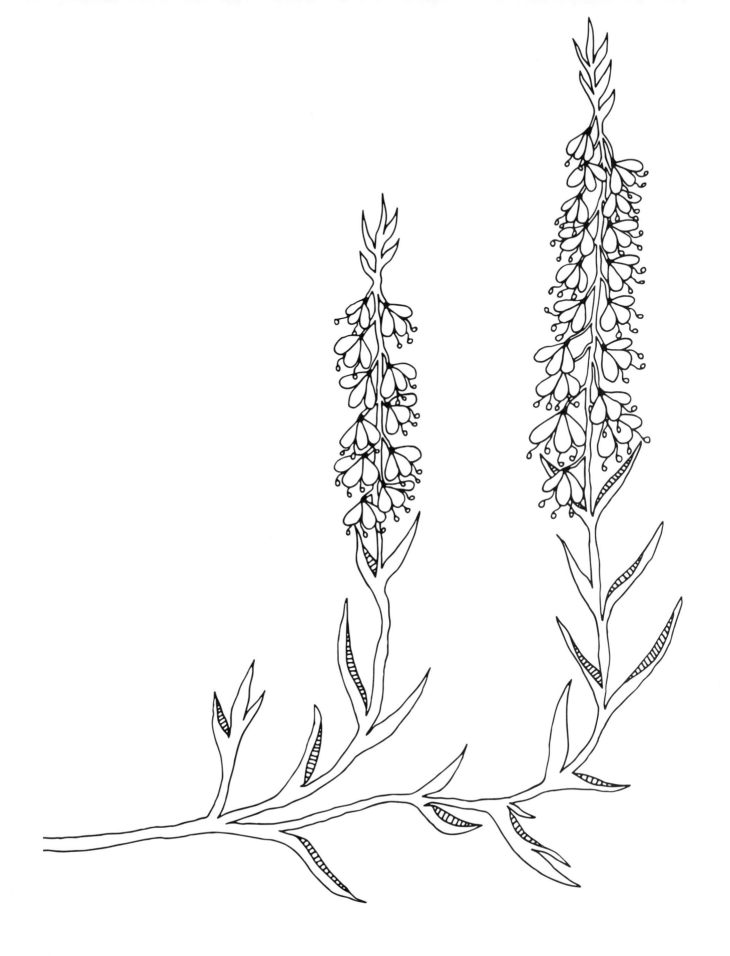

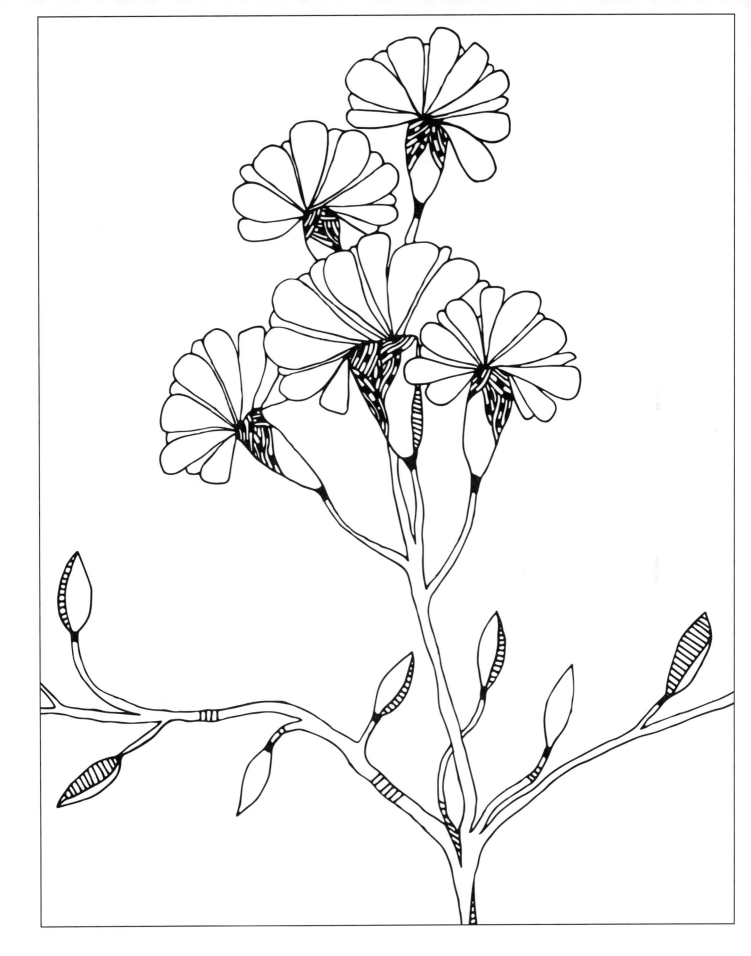

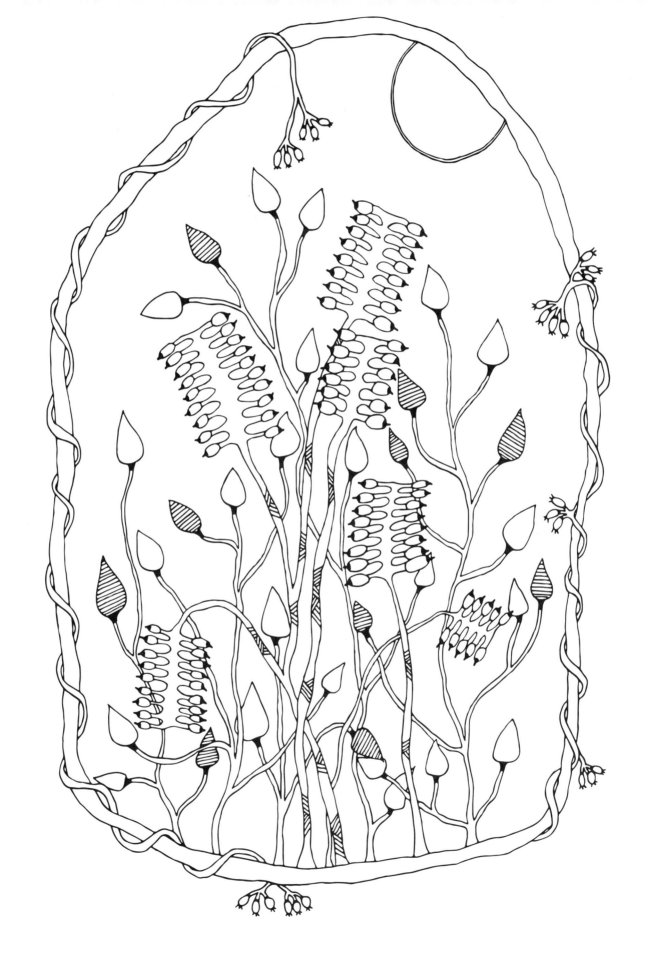

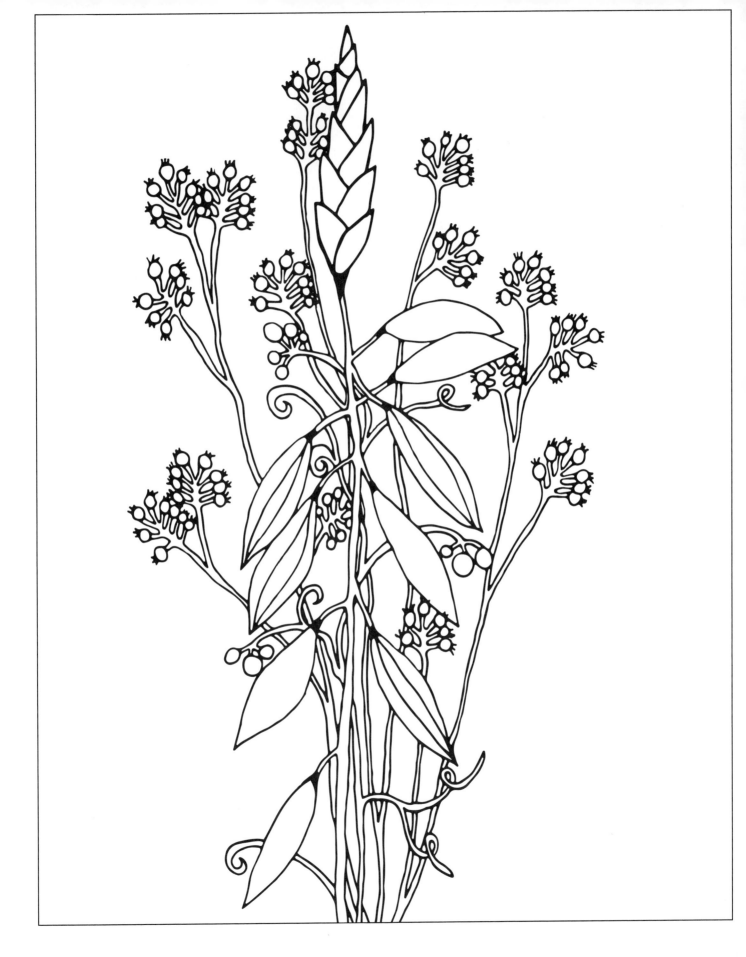

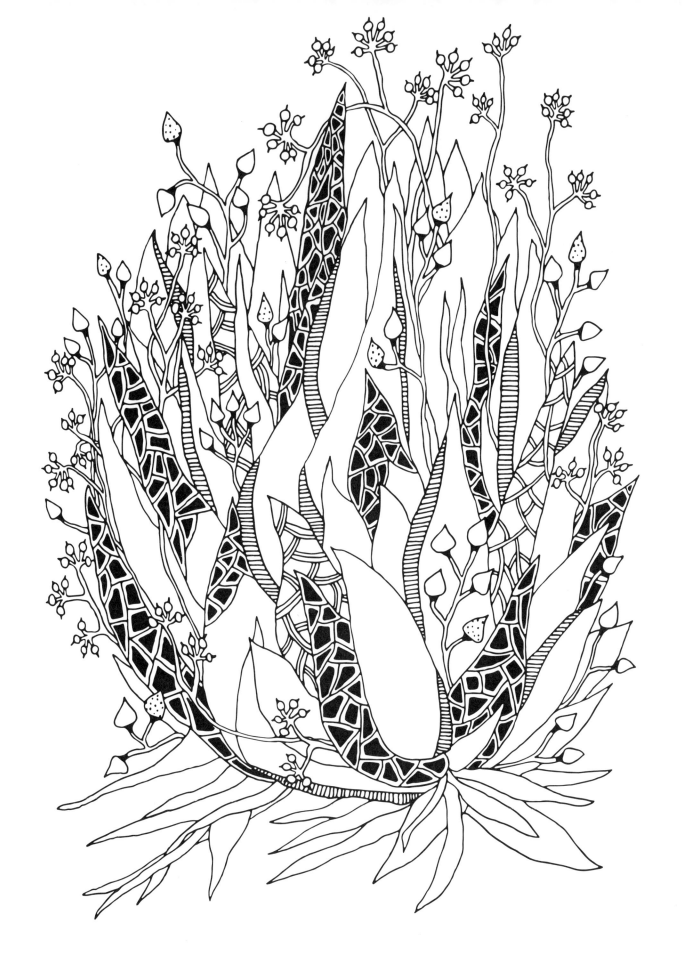

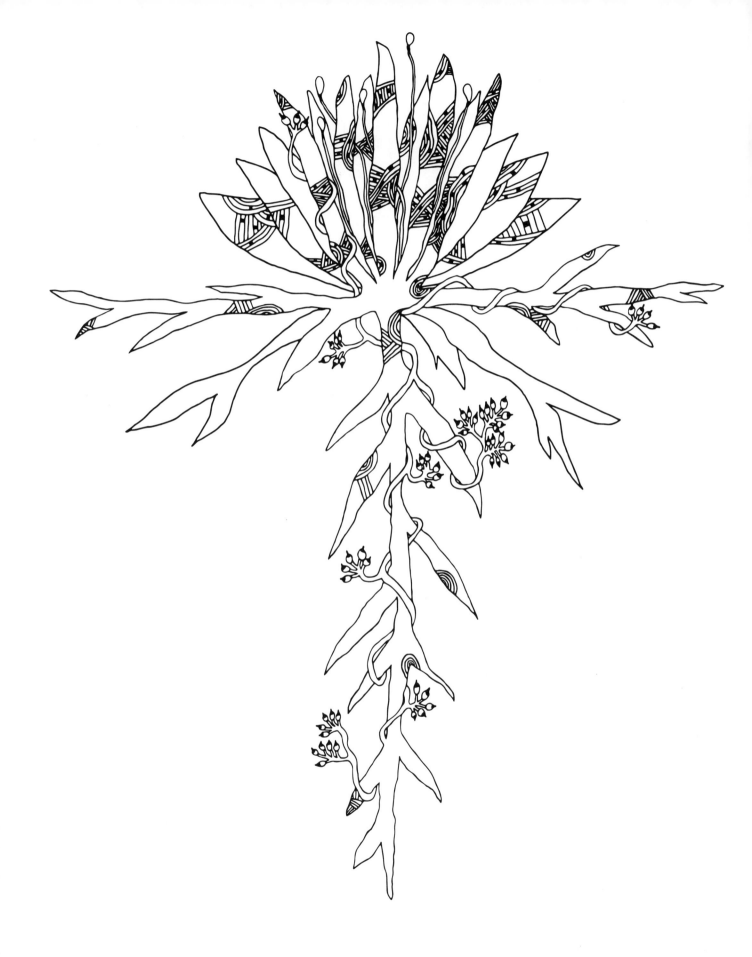

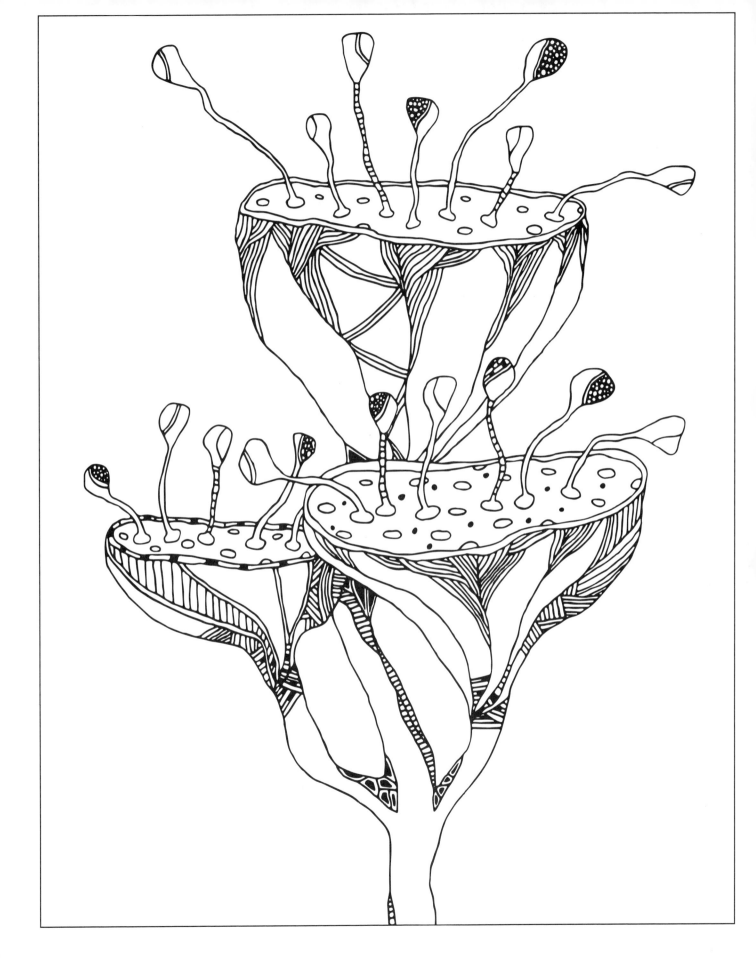

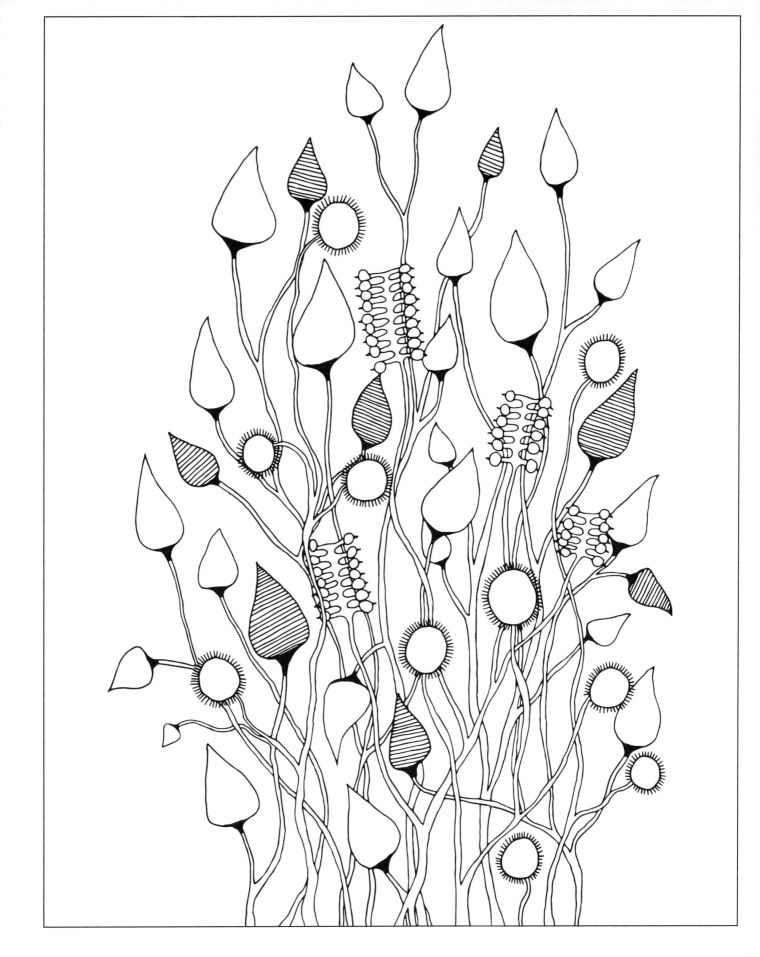

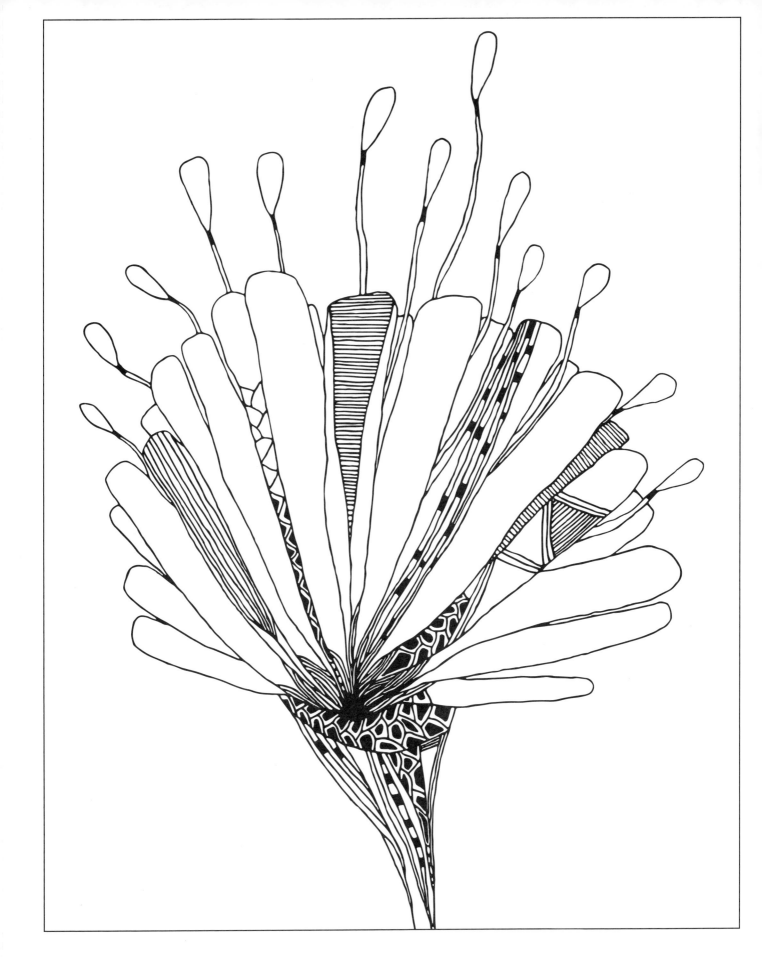

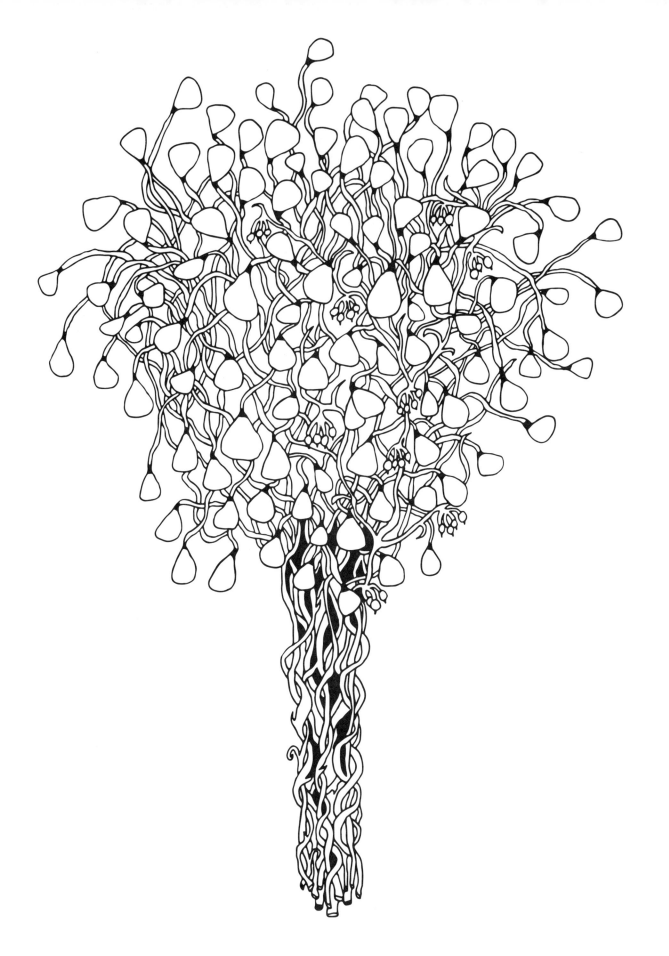

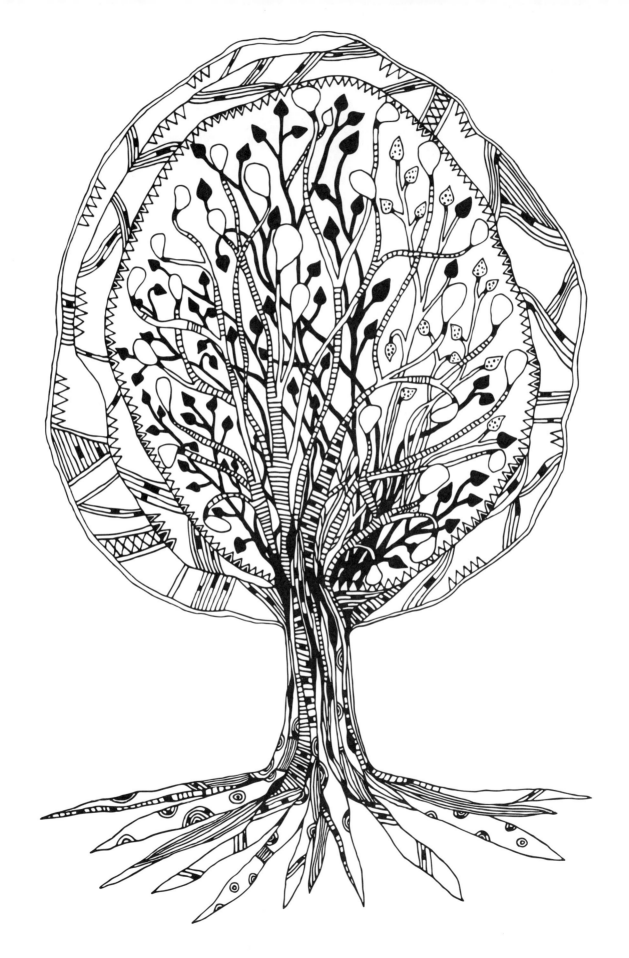

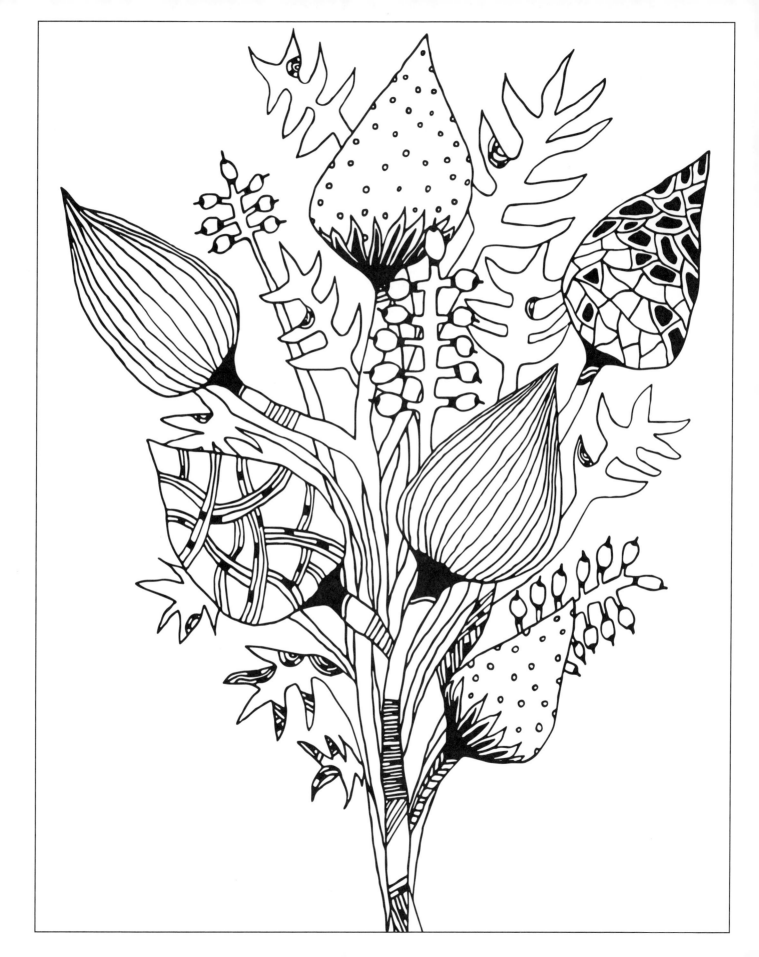

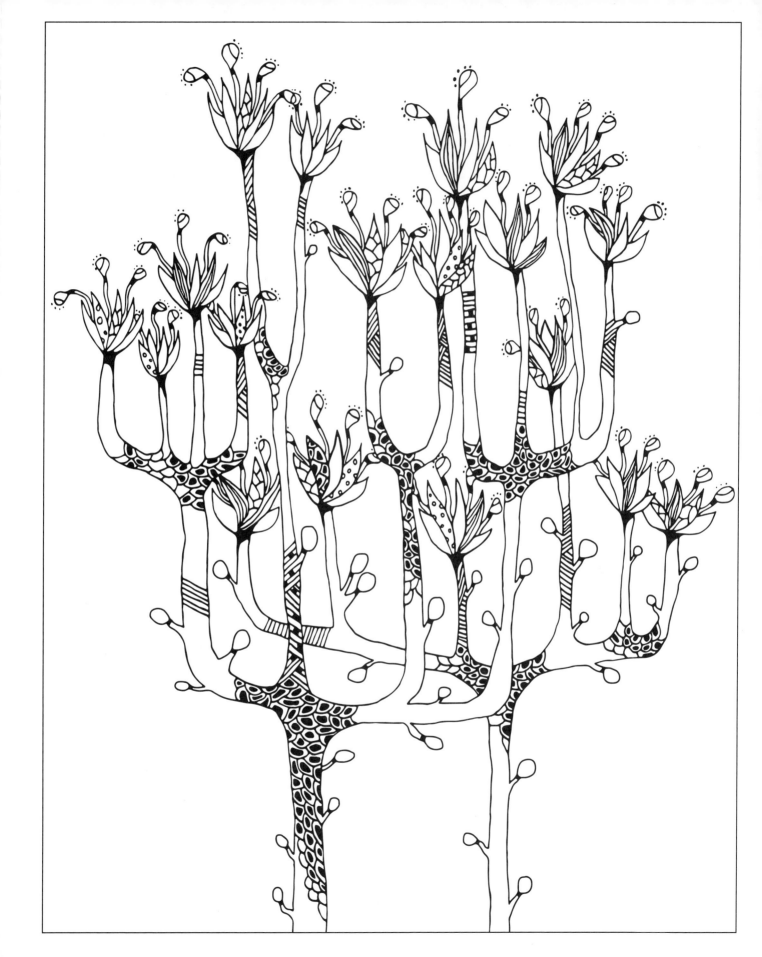

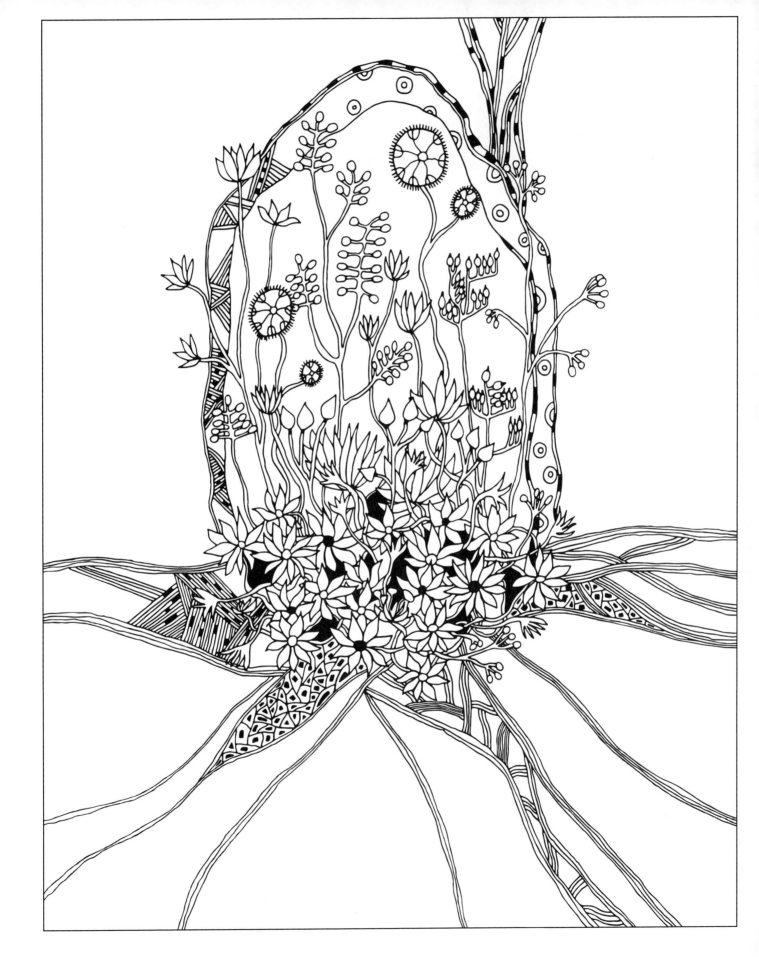

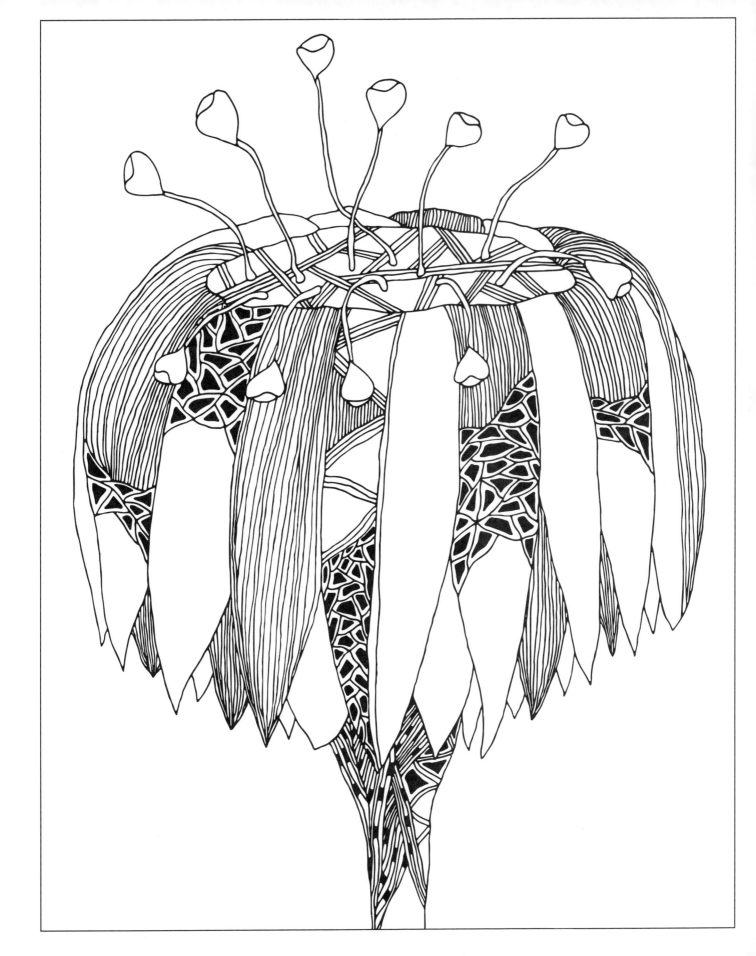

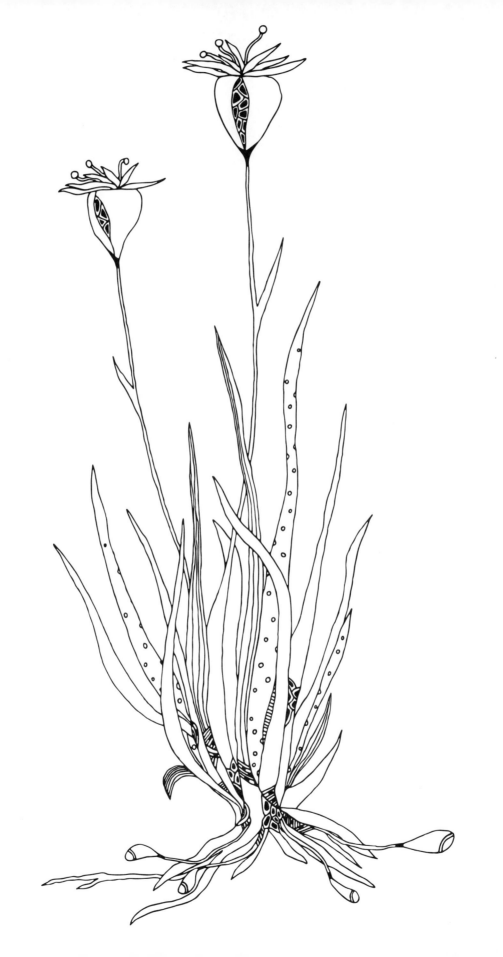

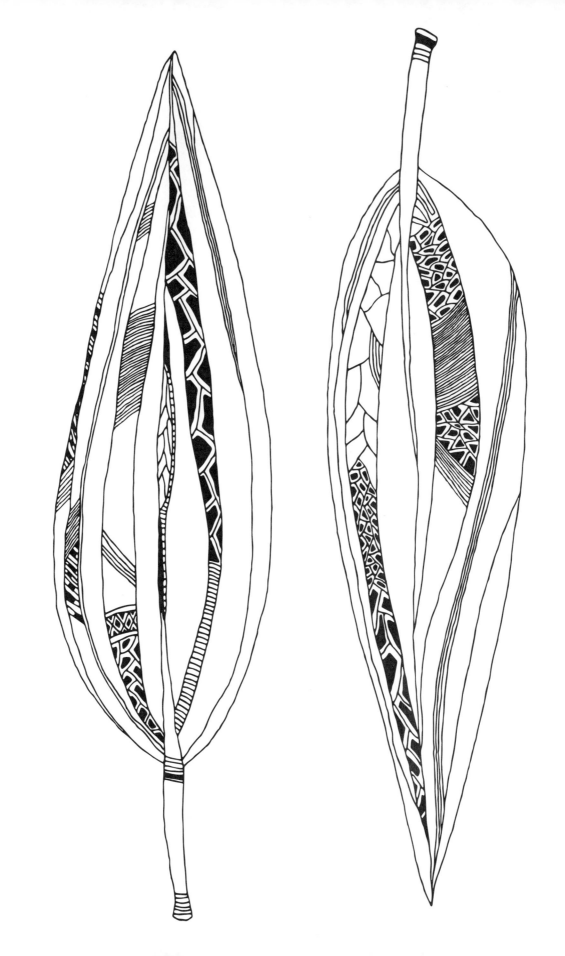

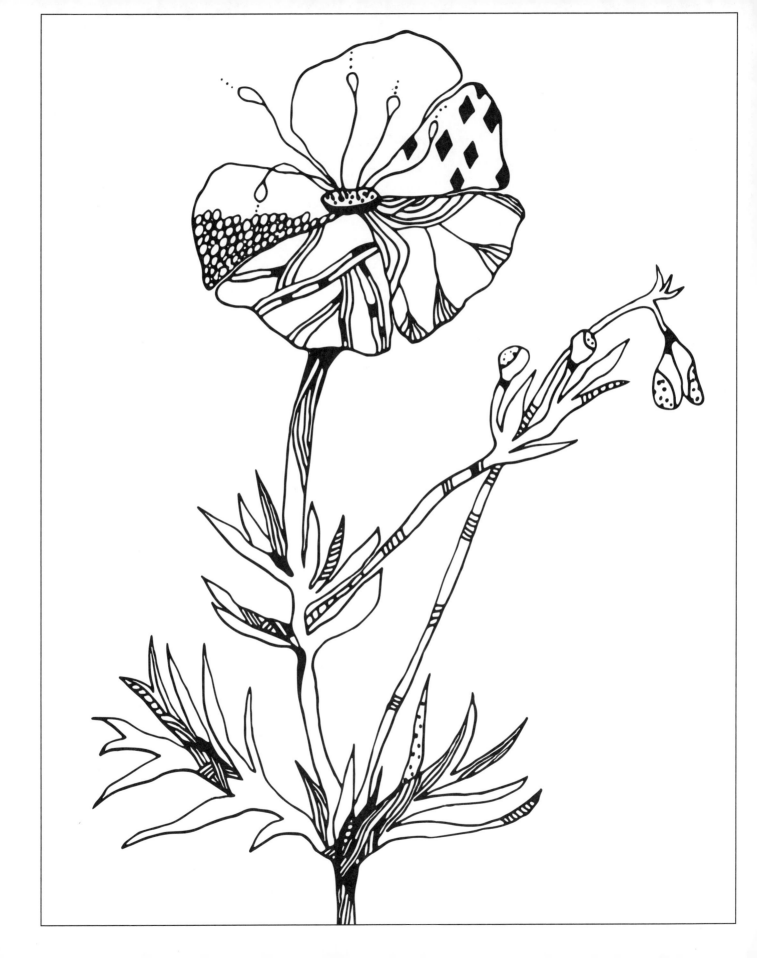

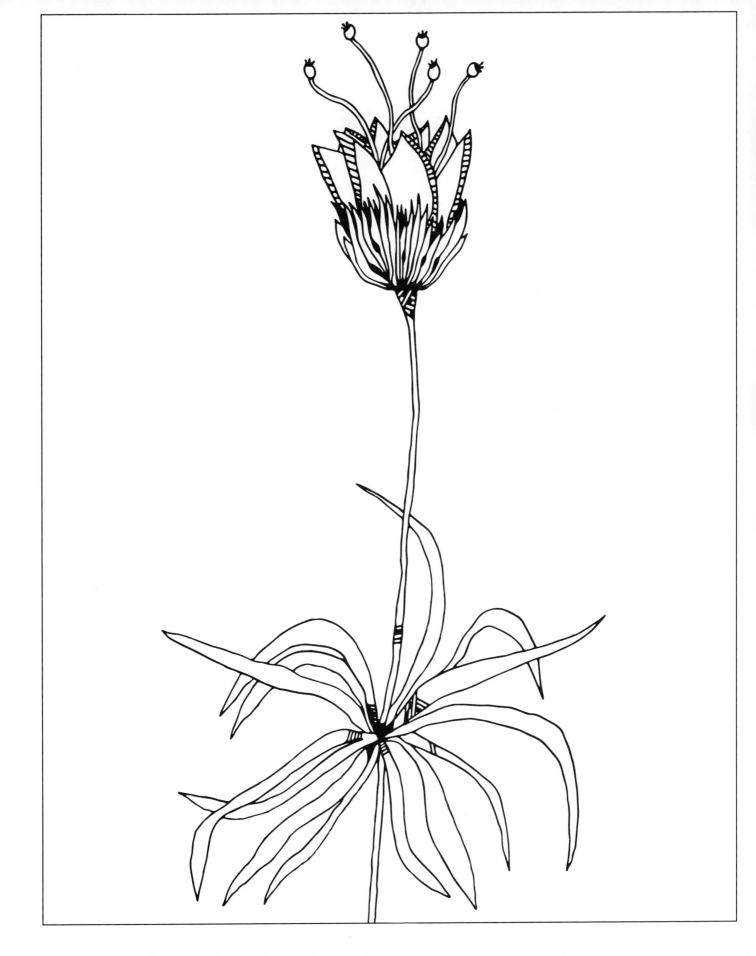

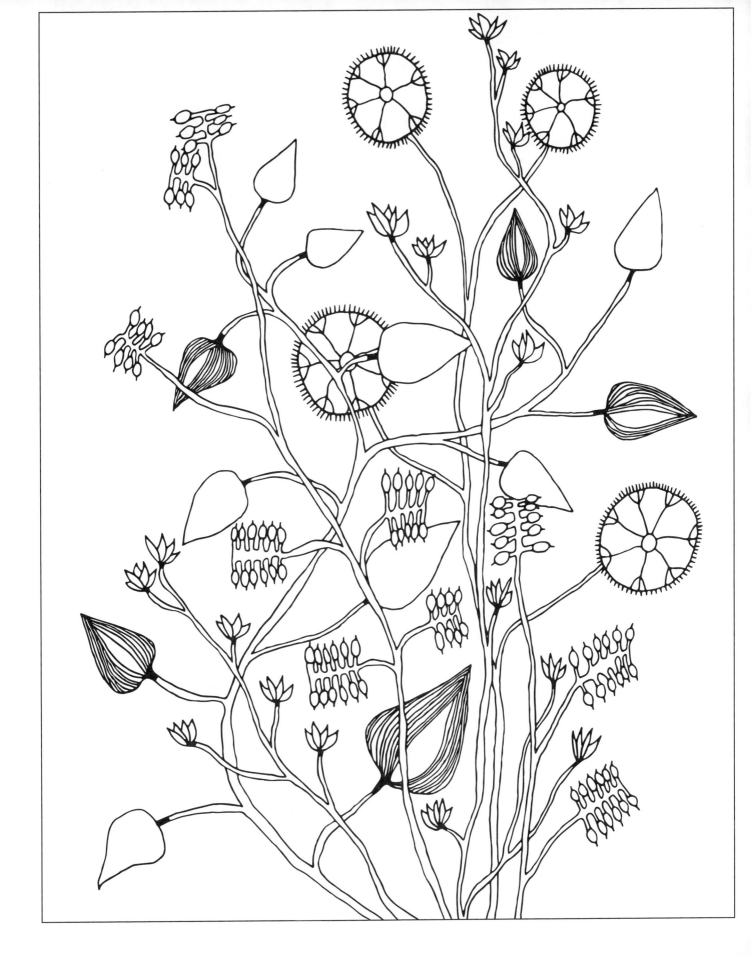

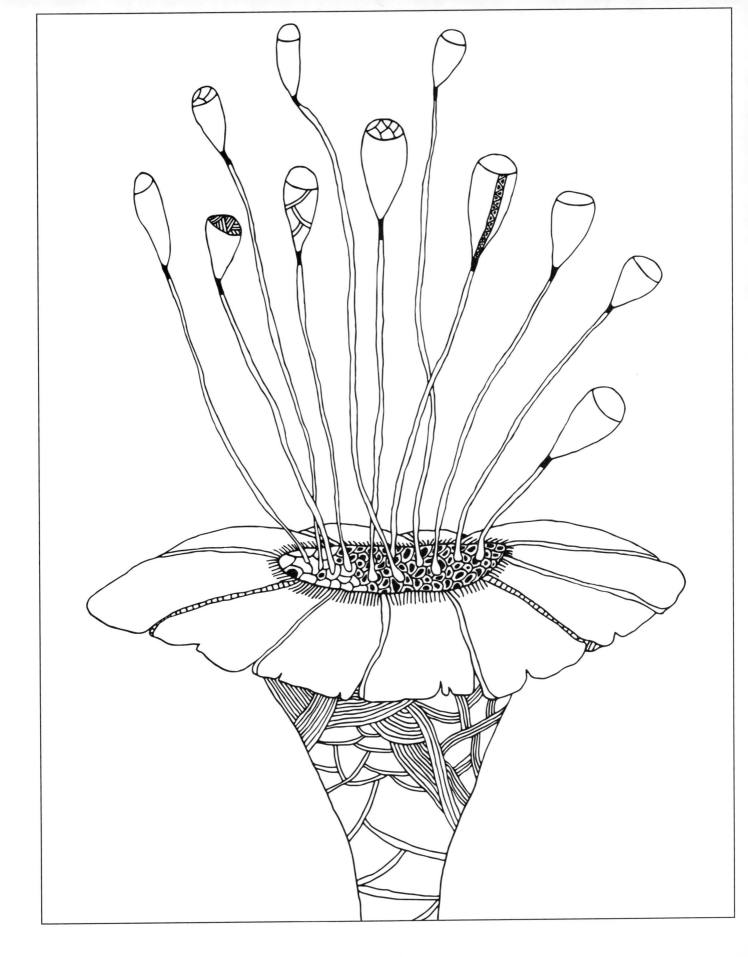

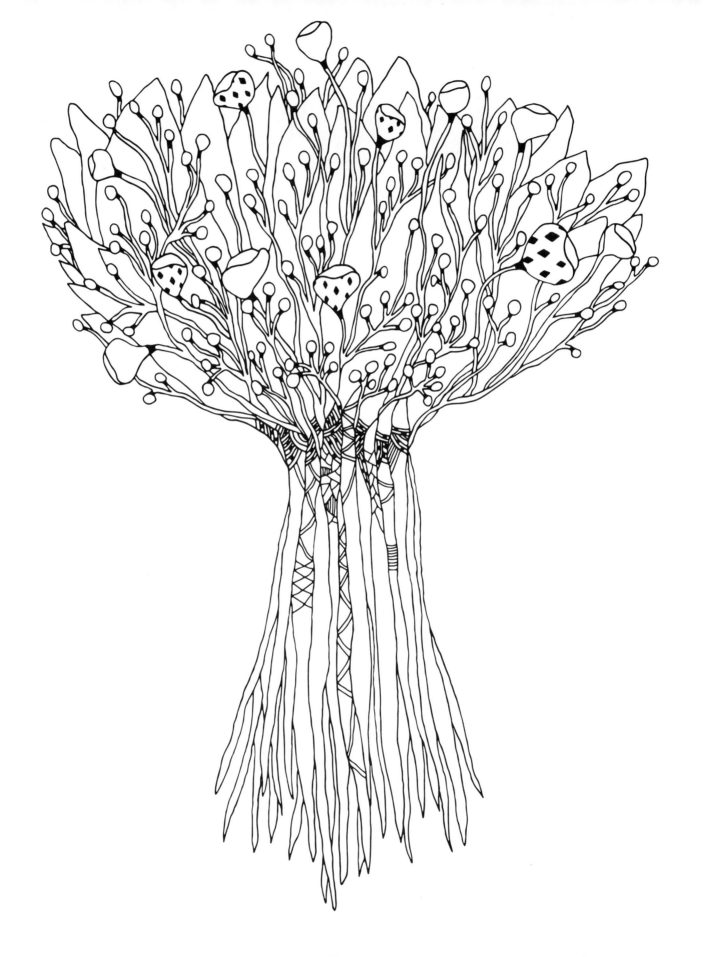

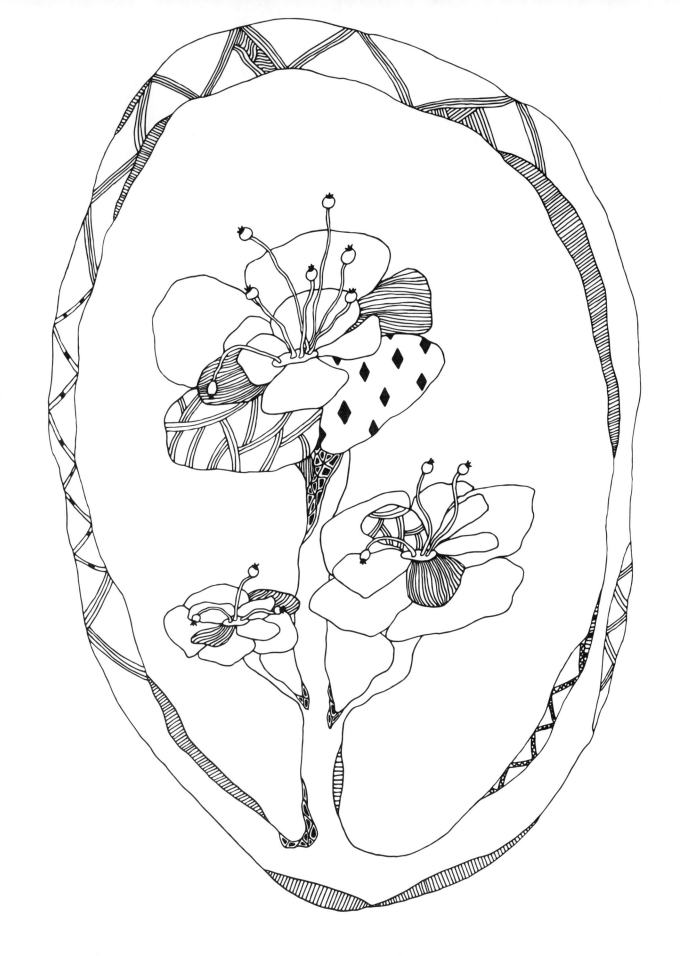

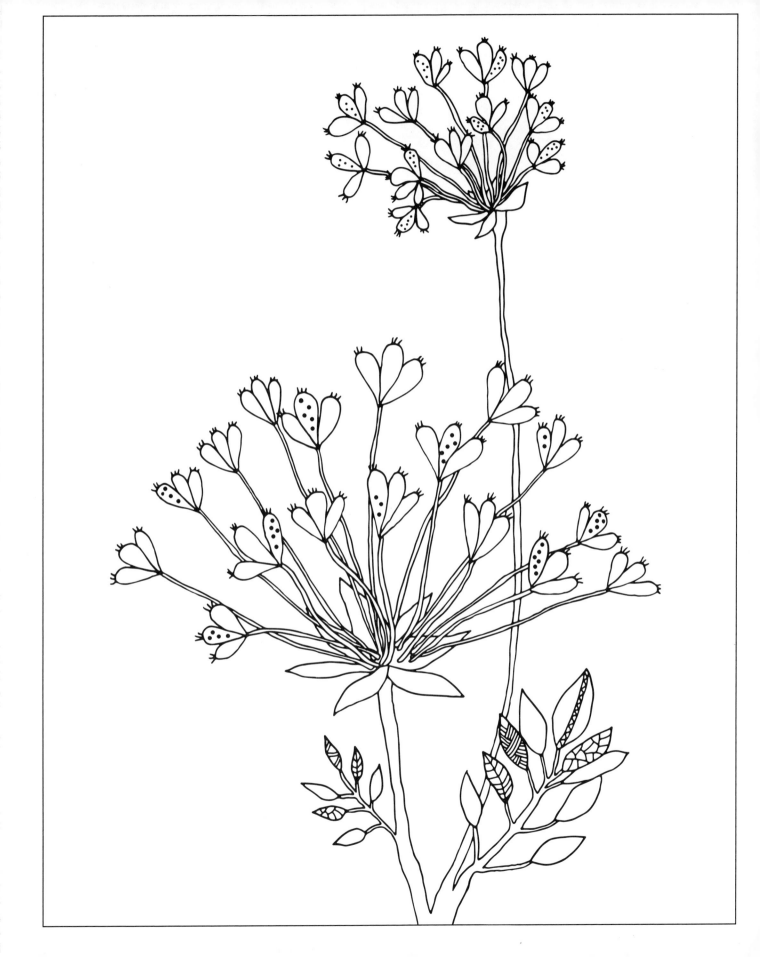

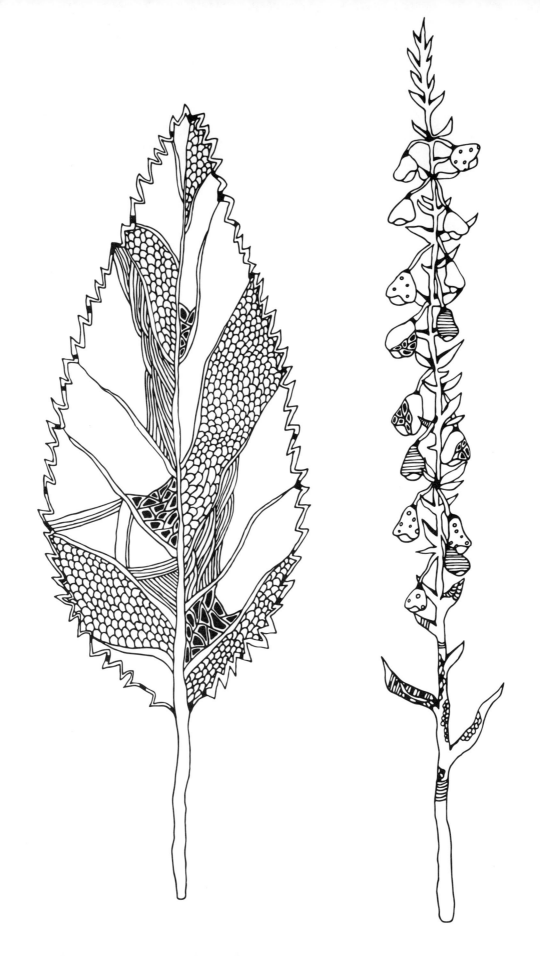

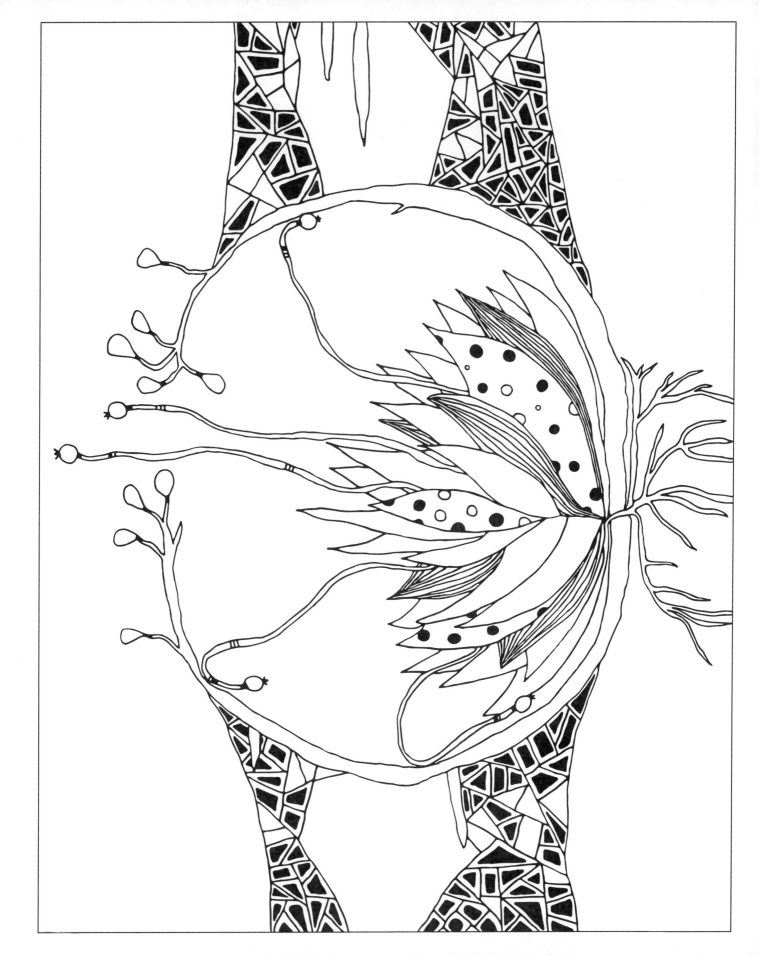

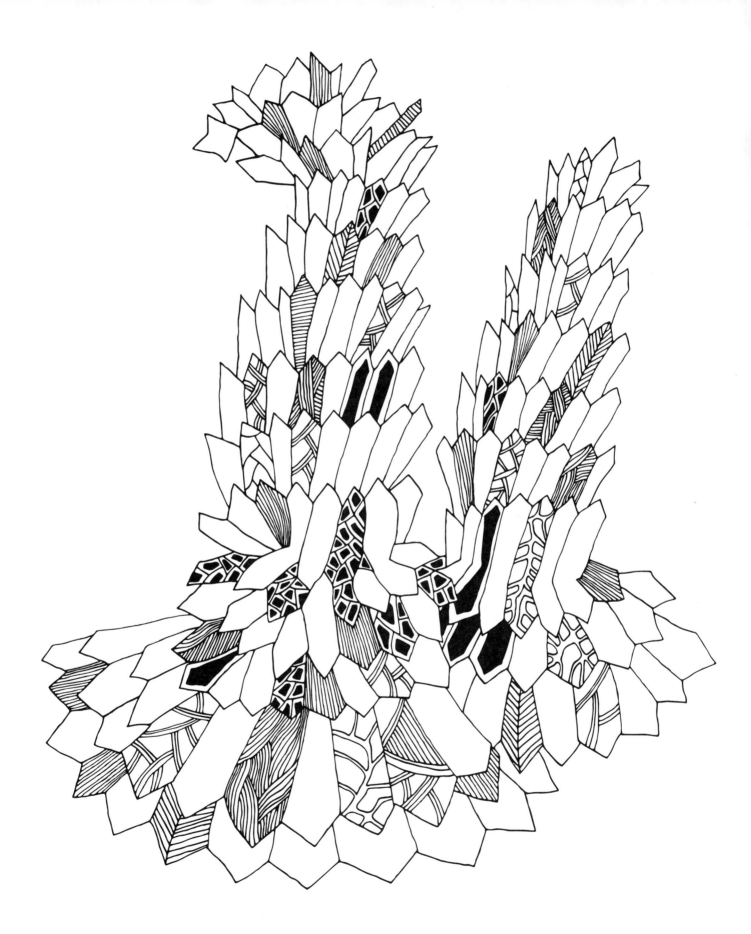

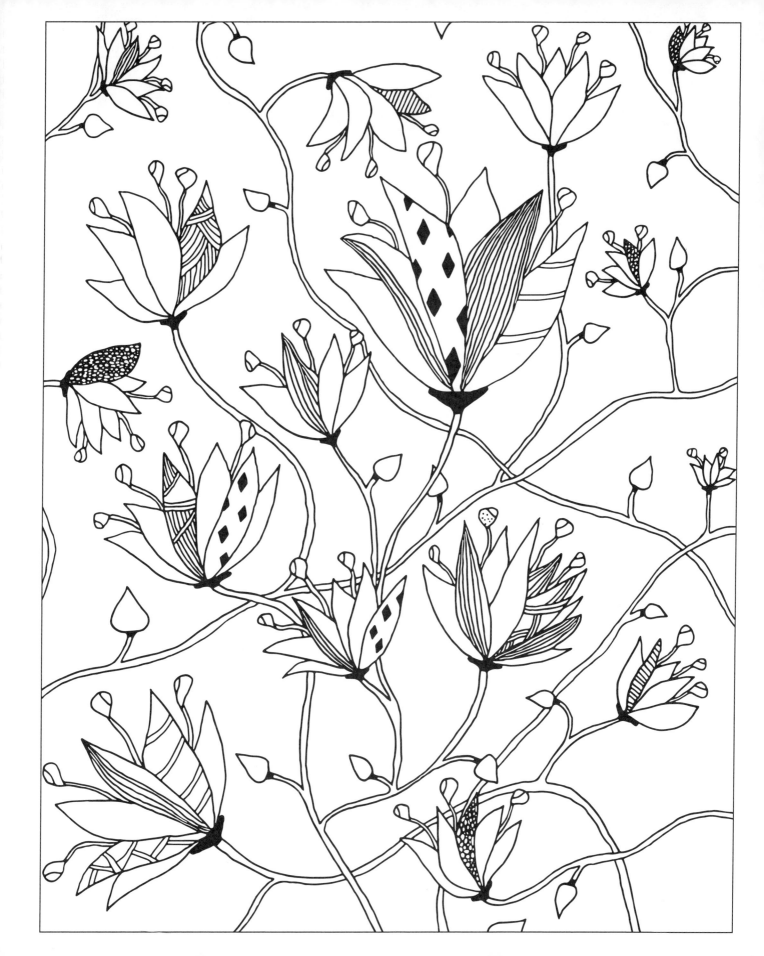

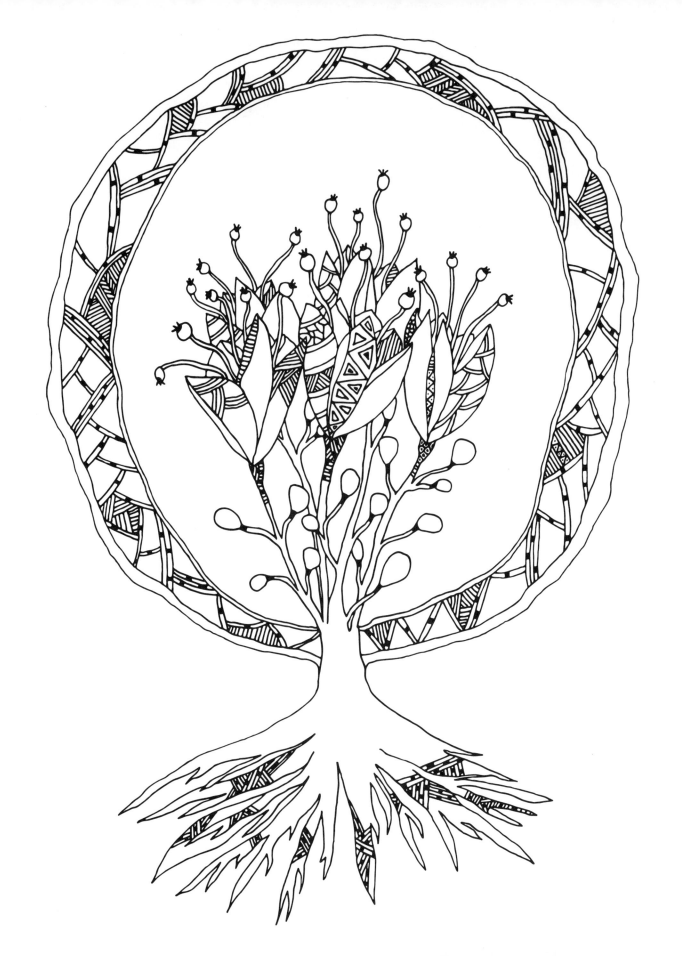

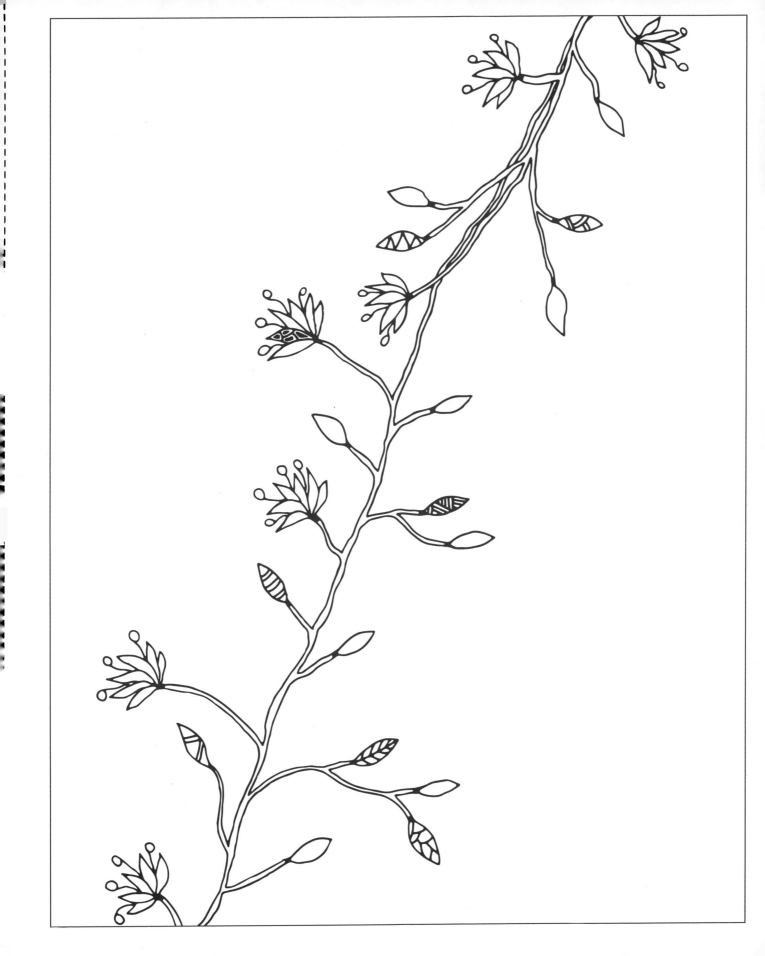

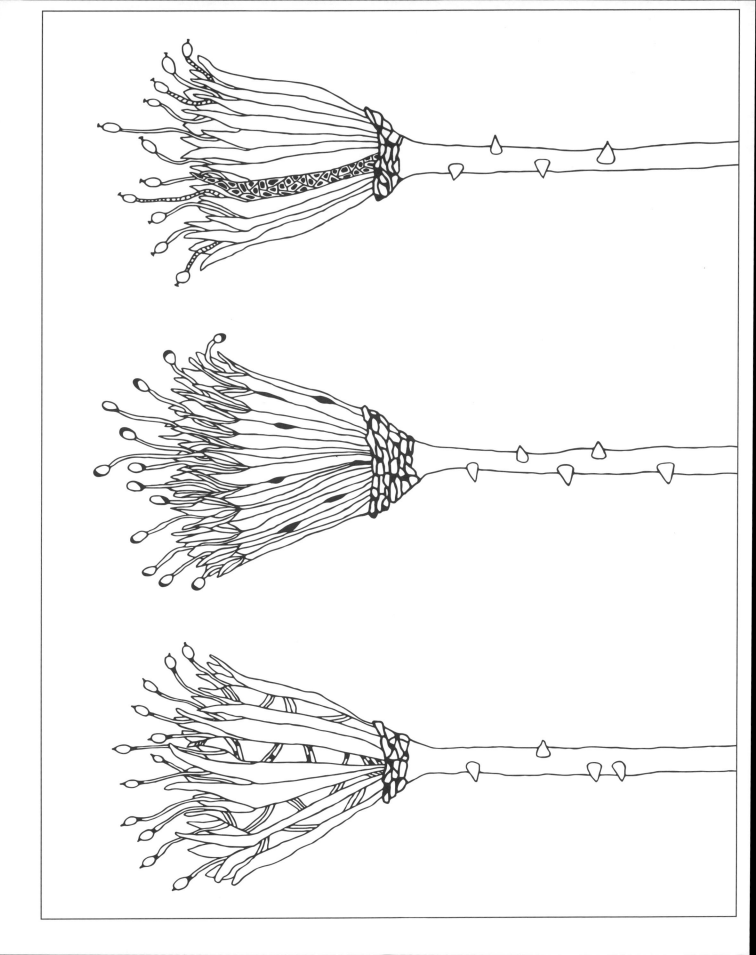

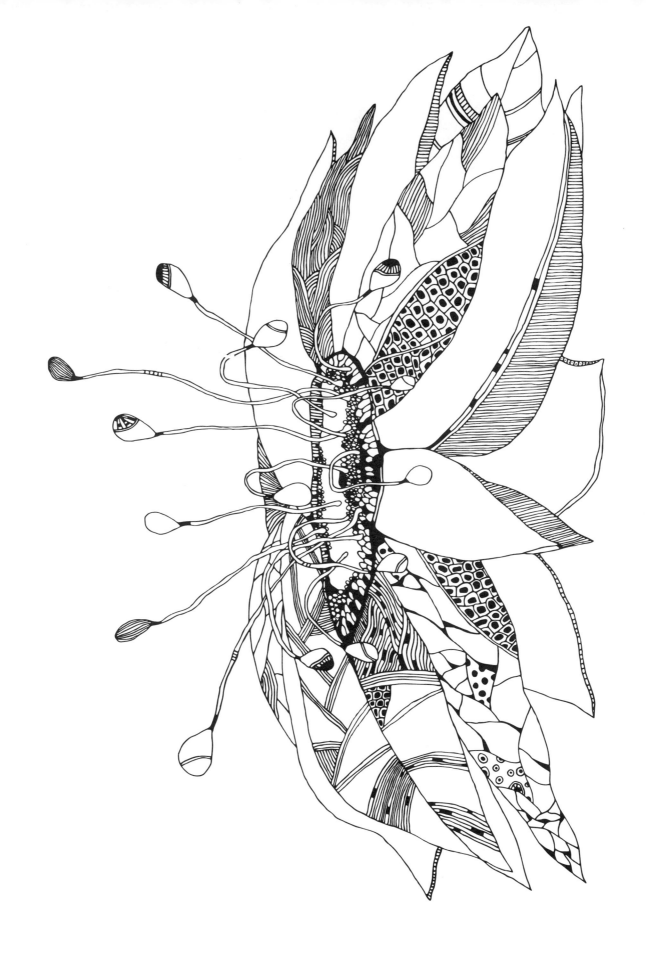

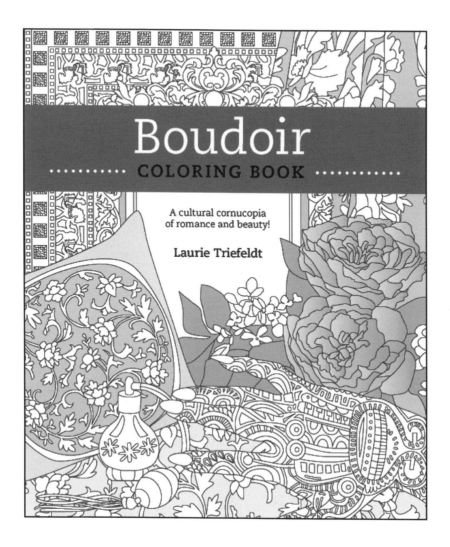

Every woman needs a room of her own, a meditative space where the bustle of the outside world can be forgotten. Find your private place in the enchanting world of *Boudoir Coloring Book*. Designed by renowned artist Laurie Triefeldt, *Boudoir Coloring Book* offers hours of creative absorption in a personal world of calmness and beauty. These intricate images of elegant ladies, vanity tables, perfume, make up, and flowers will transport you to a place of rest and relaxation. Thick, high-quality paper, printed on only one side, gives you a smooth, firm coloring surface with no bleed-through, and perforated pages let you share and preserve your creative work. Discover your own personal world in the pages of *Boudoir Coloring Book*.

Available at bookstores, online retailers, and at www.QuillDriverBooks.com.

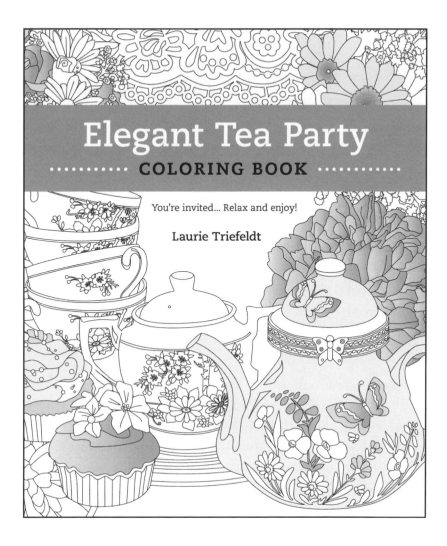

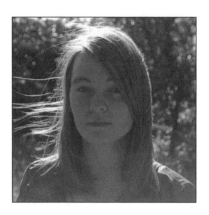

Sigita Alekne

I was born in 1985 in the town of Telsiai, in northwest Lithuania. I grew up between the homes of my parents and my grandparents, who lived in the countryside. So I felt close to nature as a child and I have always been fascinated by its beauty and the calmness it brought me.

As I was growing up, the people of Lithuania experienced great change, and it had an impact on everybody. The collapse of the Soviet Union in 1990 liberated people. However, there was still a lot of confusion, and even though I was a child I observed many injustices around me. I felt some kind of need inside me to do something about it, to do something "right," so I entered law school at Mykolas Romeris University in Vilnius, and I received a Master's degree in Human Rights in 2011. I started working for the national LGBT rights organization, one of the oldest NGOs established in Lithuania since its independence. Working in this field has been quite a challenge at times, since human rights, especially LGBT rights, are still not well understood or accepted by politicians and the general public of Lithuania. However, this experience taught me a lot and I am happy to see that things are slowly changing for the better.

I worked for the organization for almost five years. Then this year I decided to resume work on some of my personal projects, so I left my job and dedicated myself to drawing, which I feel great a passion for. My drawings caught the attention of the Lithuanian publisher Alma Littera, and they will be publishing my work in the form of a coloring book, postcards, and a notebook in 2016. I am continuing to work on my drawing and other creative projects.

I am recently married and we have a lovely cat, and all three of us live in an apartment right next to the Old Town of Vilnius.

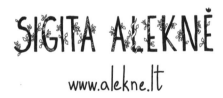

www.alekne.lt